EVERYDAYCOOK

PRODUCED BY

Alton Brown

PHOTOGRAPHED BY

Sarah DeHeer

STYLED BY

Meghan Splawn

BALLANTINE BOOKS NEW YORK

Published in the United States by Ballantine Books,
an imprint of Random House,
a division of Penguin Random House LLC, New York.

BALLANTINE and the HOUSE colophon are registered
trademarks of Penguin Random House LLC.

ISBN 978-1-101-88571-0
Ebook ISBN 978-1-101-88572-7

Photographs by Sarah De Heer

Printed in the United States of America on acid-free paper

randomhousebooks.com

9 8 7 6 5 4 3 2 1

First Edition

Book design by Liz Cosgrove

CONTENTS

RANDOM NOTES IN LIEU OF A PROPER INTRODUCTION

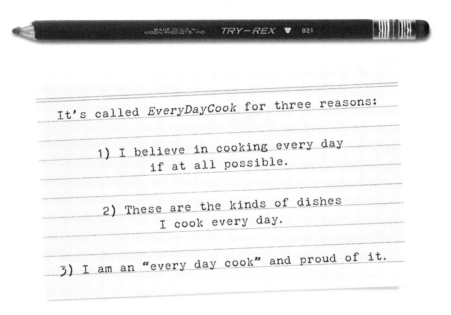

It's called *EveryDayCook* for three reasons:

1) I believe in cooking every day if at all possible.

2) These are the kinds of dishes I cook every day.

3) I am an "every day cook" and proud of it.

Technically, this is my eighth book, but in some ways it feels like the first because (like it says on the cover) this time it's personal. The recipes herein were not created to illustrate scientific principles or flesh out story points for a TV show. These dishes were concocted because somebody (usually me) was hungry. Sure, some of the lessons learned while cranking out fourteen years of *Good Eats* episodes informed this food, as did discoveries made while hosting hundreds of *Iron Chef America* episodes. And yet, these dishes are personal. This is what I eat and, more important, what you'd probably eat if you came over for breakfast, lunch, dinner, or anytime in between. Do I have more? Maybe . . . but that's another book.

Concerning the order of things: I didn't arrange this book by time of day to be different or difficult, it's just how my brain functions. If it helps at all you can flip through to the back and consult a list that sorts things by ingredient and by meal. But I do hope you'll actually consider pasta for breakfast because that should be a thing.

Besides the recipes, there are a few sections you might peruse at your leisure. The Pantry area tours some less-than-common ingredients that have emerged as stock players in my day-to-day cooking, while the Hardware pages profile a few of the tools I would have a hard time living without. Finally, in the Methods section I share my particular ways of doing some particular things such as working with pressure cookers or cleaning cast iron, something that's become a bit of an obsession of late.

Oh, and a word about measurements and the like: Despite the grumblings of my editor, I've decided to quantify these recipes the way I do in real life. That is, they are not standardized according to any particular methodology. For instance: I combine weights (metric no less) with standard volumetric measurements, that is, tablespoons, in the same recipe. I do this not because I'm crazy but because it's practical. I weigh when it matters, and when it doesn't, I don't. However, when I do weigh, it's always metric because . . .

I *hate* fractions.

I also hate working with decimal points, and that's the nice thing about grams. No one ever says 18.4 grams unless they're weighing out something that's controlled either by local/state/federal laws or by international treaties. Now, I know that there are those of you who say food isn't worth the trouble of purchasing a decent, multi-format digital scale with tare function (allows weights to be zeroed out), but you would be flat-out wrong. You can purchase a great scale for well under a hundred dollars, and I believe that no purchase could be more beneficial to your cooking game. And trust me, if a recipe herein states a weight and you decide not to weigh . . . well, don't come crying to me, buster.

Other than that, nothing too unusual here. Most of the recipes are written in a fairly informal, narrative style, so please just take a few minutes to read them through before you go tearing around the kitchen gathering up stuff. But when you do go forth to gather, remember . . . organization will set you free.

About the photos: This is the first time that I've actually shot food specifically for a book, and unlike most authors who are more than happy to hand the chore off to a specialist, I'm a bit of a control freak, so I insisted on keeping the production in-house. And to make things even more challenging, I insisted we shoot every photo from directly overhead with an iPhone 6s Plus. That's right . . . we shot the whole book with a phone.

As for plates, silverware, glasses and all that jazz, that's all my personal stuff and yes, I really eat with surplus U.S. Army forks; yes, that's a Mercury hubcap on page 177; yes, I have carried potato chips around in a briefcase; yes, that's my car on page 38 (his name is Klaus); and if you've never eaten french fries in bed, well . . . I just feel sorry for you.

Welcome to my world.

ALTON BROWN

P.S. Oh, every now and then in these recipes you'll see a little letter in a box. They're there to let you know there's more information about whatever it is either in the Hardware **H**, Pantry **P**, Bar **B** or Methods **M** section. I'm guessing you can figure out which letter represents which section.

HARDWARE

Gaze upon this photo and behold not the everyday culinary arsenal of pots and pans and spatulas and whatnot but rather the lesser-known, unsung heroes of the kitchen; items that might seem obscure, obsolescent, or downright odd, but are, in fact, indispensable to my culinary lifestyle.

1. KNIFE: I have more knives than Patrick Bateman, but this is my go-to stick. It's an acid treated carbon steel blade by Cut Brooklyn and if I took it into a light saber fight . . . I'd win.

2. TRY-REX B21 PENCIL: I forget stuff, so when I have an idea, I need a big pencil to write that idea down. I also make a lot of mistakes, so I need a big eraser. This fabulous U.S.-made device is my choice every time. I can't cook without one.

3. SPRING-LOADED TONGS: The standard-issue, nonlocking spring-loaded tongs that I'm clutching in this photo are so indispensable that many line cooks often refer to them as "my hands." I have three pairs just so I don't have to worry about losing one. And seriously . . . skip locks; they're a pain in the butt.

4. SPIDER SKIMMER: Ubiquitous in Asian kitchens, the "spider" features a long bamboo handle and a circular stainless steel strainer that resembles a spiderweb. No other tool is as useful for scooping bunches of food out of liquid, be it hot or cold. The exception, peas . . . they're just too small. I have two spiders, one large and one small. When buying, skip the fancy culinary emporium and just drop by an Asian restaurant supply.

5. STEEL WOK: I read recipes for stir-fries all the time that say, "If you don't have a wok, use a fry pan or skillet." I say, "If you don't have a wok, get a wok!" And I would add, make it steel, not cast iron or stainless or nonstick. And it shouldn't be so heavy that you can't control it easily with one hand. The wok design is all about conduction. When you concentrate heat right at the bottom, the bottom gets really hot. But, as that heat conducts up and out the ever-widening sides, it dissipates. So, when you stir-fry, you cook quickly at the bottom, then as you push food up the sides, everything slows down. It's genius. And you will be too if you buy it at an Asian restaurant supply when you pick up that spider we were talking about.

6. HEAVY-DUTY BINDER CLIPS: Sure, you can use these office supply stalwarts to close bags and the like, but I also use them positioned on pot sides to hold spoons and thermometer probes. They're also great for keeping foil pouches snugly sealed in the oven. A thousand and one uses. Get them in two sizes.

7. ELEVEN-PIECE ROUND CUTTER SET: These are the Russian nesting dolls of the culinary world, each with one rolled edge and the other a relatively thin cutting edge. The obvious chores would include cutting various forms of pastry for tarts, biscuits, doughnuts, and cookies. But they can also help you up your plating game. Ever been to a restaurant where there is a perfect disk of, say, beef tartare resting over an equally perfect flat of horseradish custard? No? Well one of these babies probably served as the mold. Oh, and when you want a perfect hole cut in bread for toad in the hole, look no further.

8. AEROPRESS COFFEEMAKER: I don't have a coffee problem. Honestly.

Okay, I have a coffee problem, but it's not really a problem as long as I continue to get coffee. Although I prefer espresso shots expertly pulled from machines that go for five figures, truth is, I don't have one of those machines so I use this. Is it true espresso? No . . . it produces about eight ounces of very strong coffee that, depending on the grind, is espresso-esqe. But it costs about thirty dollars and, along with an electric kettle, makes a very portable coffee kit. I started using it when I was touring my variety show, and when I got home, I just kept going. "Ah!" I hear you say. "But is this not a unitasker, which you deplore?" Actually, it's not. I use it to brew tea and various tisanes and elixirs, so back off.

9. KYOCERA CERAMIC MANDOLINE: Once upon a time I didn't take ceramic blades seriously. But then I did a charity event and the gift bag contained one of these. About six months later, when one of the ten screws on my pricey metal mandoline cross threaded, I broke it out. It offers only four cut thicknesses, .5, 1.3, 2, and 3 millimeters, but the adjustment device is cunningly simple and it's as sharp now as it was a year ago.

10. STAINLESS STEEL RULER: Measuring in the kitchen is a lot like casting a movie; get it right and the rest is easy. And yet for some reason, you don't see too many rulers in kitchens. Well, this old Fiskars has been with me for pretty much ever, and I use it constantly. If I have to roll out a dough, I measure and draw the desired shape out on parchment paper first using this. I need a straight line, there it is. I also use it in pots quite a bit. Need to reduce a liquid by half, just measure its depth then check periodically as the liquid level drops. Just measure the depth of your liquid, then check periodically as the liquid reduces. And this ruler is even dishwasher safe!

11. MICRO-RASP GRATER: This is the original-issue Microplane, and though the producer tries hard to improve on it . . . alas, perfection is tough to surpass. Perfect for grating hard cheeses, spices like nutmeg, hard chocolate, lemon zest, and garlic. (Later models have handles . . . we don't need no stinkin' handles.)

12. SHOP BRUSH: This thing came from a hardware store, and I use it for cleaning counters, cutting boards, whatever. I'm big on sweeping, so I typically brush everything onto the floor and then get it with a regular broom. Oh, it's also good at sweeping excess flour off bread, crumbing cakes, and stuff like that.

13. COLLAPSIBLE STEAMER BASKET: If you look closely, you'll notice this is a three-level collapsible steamer basket called the Steel Lotus. It's an extremely useful device, but you can't buy one. Sorry. You can however build one by removing the center posts from three folding steamer baskets and threading them in sequence onto a piece of appropriate-diameter threaded stock from the hardware store. A nut placed

above and below each steamer will keep them in place. The entire endeavor will run you about twenty bucks.

14. ELECTRIC KETTLE: I've waxed rhapsodic about these things in the past, but honestly, if I need to heat water, even if it's eventually going into a pot, I heat it in an electric kettle. Now that pour-over coffee is all the rage, manufacturers are offering models that can be set for specific temperatures, not just boiling. I don't have one of those yet, but you can totally send me one if you want.

15. CHEESECLOTH: Although this loose-weave cotton fabric can be finished in various ways for use in garments, the most famous culinary application is straining cheese curds and lining cheese molds. I also use several layers in a hand sieve for fine straining. It's also perfect for making spice sachets and tea bags and the like. When I salt a rib roast for aging, I typically wrap it in at least three layers of cheesecloth to keep the surface from toughening during the process.

16. PROPANE TORCH: Although small, handheld butane torches have become popular culinary items with the crème brûlée boom of the 2000s, due to a host of chemical factors (flame temperature and velocity), butane torches are essentially glorified cigar lighters. If you want to produce a real char on any surface, get thee to a hardware store and purchase a decent propane torch like the ones used by plumbers and welders. Not only will you be able to melt sugar without

heating the custard beneath, when you need to light a fire, or braze a pipe, you'll have this multitasker at hand.

17. VINTAGE ICE CREAM SPADE: I know a lot of cooks who have favorite spoons that they reach for when saucing, serving, tasting, stirring, ladling, basting, and so on. This is mine. Yes, it is old, and yes, it's meant for ice cream. I don't care. It fits my hand, its handle is positioned at the perfect angle, and I find its wide, relatively shallow bowl perfect for well . . . me.

18. DIGITAL SCALE: If you want to be a better baker, weigh *everything*. Okay . . . maybe not everything but darn near everything. Today's scales are easy to use, inexpensive, precise, and accurate (and no, those aren't the same thing). If I'm scaling, say, the pizza dough on page 180, I literally park the work bowl on the scale, hit the tare function to zero out its weight, and repeat with every ingredient. Now, I'm probably not going to weigh out a teaspoon of vanilla extract or half a teaspoon of cayenne pepper (you'd need a pharmaceutical scale for that), but if I can easily weigh it, I probably will. This model is made by Oxo, and I like it because its readout actually pops out. It's connected on a wire for easy reading when working with large containers.

19. BOARD SCRAPER/DOUGH KNIFE: I know there are people out there who live without these, but honestly I don't know how. Yes, they're meant for cutting large blobs of dough into manageable pieces, but they're equally adept when it comes to scooping up and conveying, say, a pile of chopped onions to the pot, or scraping goo or crumbs or whatnot off your counter or cutting board. If I had a third hand, I'd be holding one in this photo.

20. KITCHEN SHEARS: Knife skills not up to snuff? Why not fall back on technology you conquered in kindergarten? All you need is the proper equipment. Go for a two-piece all-metal design with interlocking pieces that can be separated for thorough washing. My favorites are made by an American company called LamsonSharp, and they'll cut through a chicken's leg bone like butter. I also keep a good pair of craft scissors around for cutting parchment and foil and the like.

21. PRESSURE COOKER: The closest thing we have to a culinary time machine. When properly employed, a pressure cooker increases the atmospheric pressure within by 10 to 15 psi (pounds per square inch), thus raising the boiling temperature of water to between 235° and 250°F. At such temperatures, foods that typically require long simmering (chickpeas, stew meats) soften in a fraction of the time. Without a pressure cooker the pho broth on page 11 would require hours rather than minutes.

22. ICE CUBE TRAY: There was a time when automatic ice makers were the playthings of the rich, like Learjets and infinity pools, and we regular folks had to fill ice cube trays with water (from the faucet, no less) and park them in our crusty, frost-ridden freezers for twelve

hours if we wanted ice. Well, today these primitive yet robust devices are just the thing for freezing into cubes a wide range of fluids from coffee and tea to stock and broth and soups or any other water-based liquid you might want to preserve and dose out an ounce at a time. You can buy two for a buck at most grocery and home stores. I own twelve … but that's me.

23. CAST-IRON PAN: Cast iron holds heat better than any other kitchen metal and if you treat it right, it'll get slicker than a mambo band. A 12-inch skillet and a Dutch oven are all you need.

24. COCKTAIL SHAKER: Believe it or not I stir most of my cocktails in a glass pitcher, but I shake most of my salad dressings in a cocktail shaker.

25. N_2O FOAMER (AKA WHIPPED CREAM SIPHON): This looks a lot like a soda siphon only instead of infusing CO_2 into water, this device infuses nitrous oxide into fatty liquids such as whipping cream, chocolate mousse, and even fondue, or, as you see on page 25, pancake batter. Just don't confuse your CO_2 cartridges with your N_2O because carbon dioxide won't whip cream and nitrous oxide won't fizz water. The foamer in the photo is made by iSi. A little more expensive than some, but worth it.

26. TELESCOPIC FORK: You need this because … Well, just trust me on this.

27. FOOD-GRADE RUBBER BANDS: I am addicted to the wide bands that come around broccoli and asparagus

and the like, especially the yellow and purple ones. For example, give your tongs extra grip for handling hot custard cups and the like by wrapping two bands on the end of each arm.

28. BOX CUTTER/UTILITY KNIFE: Unlike top-quality, artisan-made kitchen cutlery, utility knives, aka box cutters, are cheap and have relatively tiny blades … tiny *retractable* blades! That means that after cutting some string or slicing some garlic or scoring duck breasts (made possible by positioning the blade so that it's just barely sticking out), you can safely put it in your pocket. Try that with a paring knife and just see what happens.

29. PAPER PLATE: I don't know when this plain white disk crossed the line from picnic-hamper parking pad to trusted culinary cohort, but now I use paper plates as scale liners, funnels, bowl scrapers, and pie-pan liners. Five-star multitaskers to be sure.

30. MEASURING SHOT GLASS: I hate fumbling around with measuring spoons when I'm attempting to dose out small amounts of liquids. The answer: this tiny shot glass, which may hold only a fluid ounce yet is clearly indexed for teaspoons, tablespoons, ounce fractions, and milliliters. And yes, you can even do perfectly measured shots out of it.

31. PANINI PRESS: Someone gave this to me as a gift, and it sat in a closet for about two years. Then one day when I was looking for a faster way to cook a spatchcocked hen, I broke it out and, dang … that thing gave me a perfect, crisp bird in about twelve minutes, especially when I weighted it down with a heavy can. Now, as you can see by the recipe on page 156, I look to this gizmo as a front-line multitasker. My advice, though, is that if you buy one, don't go cheap. It should be heavy and all metal. And yes, you can grill a whole trout in there.

32. VACUUM BOTTLE THERMOS: The Scottish chemist James Dewar is cred- ited with inventing the vacuum flask that most Americans refer to as a Thermos. The device takes advantage of the fact that heat prefers to move from one body to another by means of either conduction or convection. By placing a liquid into a vessel that is suspended inside another vessel with a partial vacuum in between, heat literally has nowhere to go and the contents remain either hot or cold for a very long time indeed. I find a good Thermos is absolutely the best way to keep sauces such as hollandaise hot between cooking and serving. Oh, and it will keep coffee hot too.

33. HEAVY-DUTY ALUMINUM FOIL (AKA THE KING OF THE MULTI-TASKERS): I made a saucepan out of this stuff once . . . and a ladle, and a roasting rack, and a grill, and a smoker, a full-size F-15, and a spork. I also use it to cover the smoke alarm in my apartment when I cook steak, but let's keep that between us.

THERMOMETERS

If cooking is defined as the application of heat to food (and it is), then it follows that the concerned cook would desire to know as much as possible about how much heat was actually in said food. For that we have thermometers, and I keep four types in my kitchen at all times.

34. INSTANT-READ THERMOMETER: Wherever you stick the tip, that's where it reads. Some models are faster than others, so I count to three before reading the display. And remember, it's typically the tip that does the measuring, not the entire length of the probe. Look for a backlight and a switch that allows for reading in Celsius or Fahrenheit. Oh, and you want a range from 32° to at least 350°F, if possible.

35. REMOTE PROBE THERMOMETER: I can't roast anything without one. The probe goes into the target food, the food goes into the oven, and the thin lead wire (heat- and crushproof) runs out the door to the base unit, which tells you what's going on in the oven. Look for a model that allows you to set an alarm when your target temp is attained. Some models have probes and attachments to use as fry thermometers, but I've never seen one that I like as much as an old-fashioned . . .

36. LIQUID BULB CANDY/FRY THERMOMETER: Although I am a fan of digital thermometers, no piece of circuitry will ever replace my bulb thermometer. Not only does this thing clamp perfectly onto a pan, that rising column of liquid (I still have a few mercury models) shows you not only what temperature your syrup or fry oil is with stunning accuracy, it shows you the trend, that is, the speed at which the temperature is either rising or falling, and sometimes that's a more important factor than the temperature itself.

37. INFRARED OR IR THERMOMETER: These pistollike devices, which typically employ a red laser light to aid aiming, can accurately read the temperature of almost any surface. Since it's almost impossible to know how hot a pot or pan is if "placing over high heat for 3 minutes," I've gotten in the habit of including surface temperatures when writing recipes where such information matters, as is the case with the Scrambled Eggs V3.0 on page 28. The one drawback to keep in mind: Reflective surfaces such as shiny steel pans are hard for the devices to read, which is why I use them mostly on cast-iron and dark nonstick vessels. Several companies make reliable versions, but as of this writing, I prefer those made by the American company ThermoWorks.

PANTRY
(A FEW OF MY FAVORITE THINGS)

Although I could sit here and type rhapsodic on each and every foodstuff I keep on hand in my pantry, this book would be ridiculously heavy if I did. Besides, odds are good you're familiar with things like all-purpose flour, tomato sauce, rosemary, Cap'n Crunch, and the like. So I decided to keep this list to thirty items that, albeit far from obscure, are not exactly run-of-the-mill. In any case, they're all called for in recipes herein, so let us take a few moments to consider:

The first of the ancient grains featured herein, **AMARANTH** was praised by the Aztecs who highly revered the seeds of this weed, which deliver not only protein but lysine, an amino acid that's missing from most plant foods, and explains why vegetarians like it so much. It's interesting to note that Spanish conquistadors tried to wipe amaranth out and convert the native Central Americans to wheat, but amaranth grows like the weed it is so they couldn't manage it. Because of that, the amaranth gene pool has survived intact. I've come to appreciate amaranth and amaranth flour in baking. The cookies on page 42 are addicting, but it's okay because amaranth is so darned good for you. Eat a dozen . . . go ahead.

ANCHO AND CHIPOTLE CHILES: I tend to use these two together quite a bit.

Anchos are the dried version of poblano chiles while chipotles are simply smoked and dried jalapeños. The latter are most often found in cans with adobo sauce, but those are completely different critters in my book. I like dried chiles because they'll keep forever in the pantry. I like the combination of the two because I like the fruitiness of the ancho and the smoke of the chipotle. Without either my EnchilLasagna (page 78) just wouldn't be as good. When rehydrated, they're also terrific in salsas. Oh, and if you can find the form of chipotles called ahumado, which are gray rather than brown, scoop them up . . . They're the good stuff.

ANCHOVIES: Anchovy fillets that have been salted, packed in oil, and then canned (or jarred) can deliver a serious dose of both glutamic and inosinic

acids that combine to create the savory flavors food folk call umami. And the nice thing is that it doesn't take much to do the trick. A single fillet can shake a dish up without making it taste at all "fishy." In fact, of all the folks I've served my spaghetti (see page 139) to, only one has called me on the fish. Other uses: tapenade, onion dip, beef stew, meat loaf, and yes . . . Thanksgiving turkey gravy. There! I confess!

PS: We used a can in the photo, but I actually prefer jarred versions because you can easily reseal and refrigerate what you don't use.

BLACKENING POWDER BLEND: Blackening is tricky business involving a lot of spices meeting up with extremely high heat. Get it wrong and everything tastes burned. Part of that is technique, but it's also about getting the ratios just so. There are plenty of blackening powders on the megamart shelves (seems like any chef who's so much as touched Louisiana has one), but odds are you have most of this stuff anyway, and if you don't, you should. Just remember to give this a shake before you dole it out.

I'm giving the blend to you here in parts so you can make as much or as little as you like. Just remember it's parts by volume . . . doesn't matter if it's a teaspoon or a gallon.

1 PART EACH:
Freshly ground black pepper
Cayenne pepper
Garlic powder
Ground cumin
Dried oregano
Dried thyme

2 PARTS EACH:
Kosher salt
Smoked paprika

Combine in a big jar, screw on the lid, and shake. Store in a cool place for up to 3 months.

CHIA SEED: All you have to do is attach the word *Aztec* or *Mayan* to a food and I immediately don't want to eat it. It's not that I don't like "superfoods," it's just if they're so gosh darned super, why haven't we been eating them by the shovelful all this time? This is especially true of chia, because if even a quarter of what they say about chia is true, it's all you really need to eat to live to 150. Am I intrigued by the fiber, the antioxidants, the protein? Maybe. And the fact that chia's protein is more complete than

that of flax, and that its benefits can be gleaned whether the seed is ground or not, is certainly a point of nutritional interest. But what really makes chia special is how it can be used to make Chia Pets. No, but seriously, it's the fact that the outer fibers of the seed are highly hydrophilic, allowing the seed to absorb nine times its weight in water and form a kind of gel, a curious characteristic that many "natural" beverage companies have taken advantage of. I take advantage of it too on page 22, where it helps to set almond milk into something resembling a custard. Oh, and yeah . . . it's good for you.

CRYSTALLIZED GINGER (AKA CANDIED GINGER): Chop fine and add to various cookies, cakes, breads, et cetera. Cook with sugar and water to make a syrup for use in glazes or even just iced tea, or the ginger ale on page 110. It can be used in barbecue sauce and blended into smoothies. I love the chewy texture so I just eat the stuff, and you might do the same, especially when you are traveling, because ginger's unique chemistry (compounds such as zingiberene, gingerol, zingerone) may protect against motion sickness and a host of other gastro grumbles. Whether you buy it or make your own, as long as you store it in an airtight container it will keep exactly forever.

DEMERARA SUGAR: Originally from Guyana (which was once called Demerara), this is a light brown sugar with a difference; the crystals are large, rectangular, crunchy, and dry. Most

commercial brown sugar is quite wet because it's made by blending together refined white sugar and molasses (a good thing to keep in mind if you run out of brown sugar for baking). Demerara's unique characteristics make it perfect for topping baked goods when other sugars would simply dissolve. My Apple Spice Bundt Cake (page 46) is totally made by the Demerara sprinkled onto the glaze as it cools. The sweet crunch on my Peach "Cobbles" (page 40) also comes from these mahogany gems. I would never use it as a substitute for other sugars in baking, but Demerara can go and do what no other sugar can . . . crunch.

FISH SAUCE: Imagine a fermented, concentrated liquid version of anchovies and that's fish sauce. Why? Because that's all it is. Anchovies are stacked in barrels with salt and allowed to, well . . . "rot" would probably be the correct word. Fish sauce is the liquid that's left over. I have Red Boat brand in my kitchen at all times, not because they pay me but because I love the stuff. It's funkier than a Parliament LP, and a very little goes a very long way. That said, the Pho Bo on page 11 just wouldn't be pho without it.

Side note: Opossums love fish sauce . . . that's all I'm going to say.

FIVE-SPICE POWDER: This classical mixture always contains the same five spices, but it can be mixed to many a ratio, depending on the cook. After considerable experimentation I've settled on:

(continued on page xx)

LIQUID
SMOKE

RICE STICK NOODLES

CRYSTALLIZED GINGER

FIVE-SPICE
POWDER

STAR
ANISE

GRAINS OF
PARADISE

SICHUAN
PEPPERCORNS

SMOKED PAPRIKA

MALDON SALT

RED PEPPER FLAKES

SUMAC

ANCHO AND
CHIPOTLE
CHILES

DEMERARA SUGAR

NUTMEG

MEDJOOL DATES

MUSCOVADO SUGAR

PEPITAS

FURIKAKE

LEAF LARD

KATSUOBUSHI

SARDINES

ANCHOVIES

FISH SAUCE

RED BOAT FISH SAUCE
40°N
NET 8.45 FL OZ (250 m

WHITE CORN MEAL

FLAXSEED MEAL

FLAXSEED

QUINOA

AMARANTH

WHEAT BERRIES

CHIA SEED

5 star anise pods
1 cinnamon stick
2 tablespoons fennel seeds
1 tablespoon Sichuan peppercorns (red)
15 whole cloves

I crush the anise and cinnamon roughly by wrapping them in a tea towel and smacking them with a rolling pin. Then I transfer everything to a spice grinder and pulse to a powder. Store it in airtight containment for up to ninety days. You can, of course, purchase a premade mixture, but what fun would that be? I use this in my Zissou's Buffet of Underwater Delights, page 107, but I often sneak it into pho broth as well. And you know what … it makes great ice cream too. Oh, and I rub it on ribs sometimes before I smoke them. Pork and five-spice are besties.

FLAXSEED AND FLAXSEED MEAL: It seems that flax has become the poster seed for health food pundits and gurus, given its supposed ability to combat everything from skin cancer to depression. And then there are the omega fatty acids and a fair amount of protein. Me … I just like it. Keep in mind that whole flaxseeds can pass through the gut undigested. I still like using them because I like their crunch and their flavor, but I also use the ground "meal" version, which is nutty and reminds me of old school Grape-Nuts. Remember Grape-Nuts? Oh, and I sprinkle it on peanut butter and honey sandwiches … and chocolate ice cream, which I think may well counteract any possible health benefits.

FURIKAKE: Yes, there's a lot of Asia in my pantry these days, but what can I say? Hosting a few hundred episodes of *Iron Chef America* will do that to you. Such is the case with furikake, the mixture of ground dried fish, dried seaweed, sesame seeds, and other seasonings used to flavor rice, snacks, pickles, and sushi. My thing is popcorn. I don't just sprinkle furikake … I shovel it. And that's okay because other than being rather high in sodium, it's pretty darned good for you.

PS: Some folks prefer the spicy version with wasabi, but I'm a purist.

GRAINS OF PARADISE (AKA GUINEA PEPPER, ATARE, OR ALLIGATOR PEPPER): The seeds of *Aframomum melegueta,* an African shrub related to cardamom, are available from most online spice vendors. The pyramid-shaped seeds are slightly smaller than peppercorns but … Let's put it this way: if black pepper had a mysterious, sexy and slightly naughty sister, it would be GOP. And unlike black pepper, which packs a bite but rarely any subtlety, GOP plays amazingly well with desserts, especially apples. I also like using it in my spice cake (see page 46) because no one can exactly put their finger on what it is. I like that.

HERBES DE PROVENCE BLEND: Another example of a mix that everybody has a version of. Well, I've been to France so I get one too. Again, go parts by volume.

1 PART EACH:
Dried oregano
Dried dill

Dried chervil

2 PARTS EACH:
Fennel seeds
Dried marjoram

3 PARTS EACH:
Dried thyme
Dried rosemary
Dried tarragon
Dried basil

Seal in a jar and shake. Will keep for about 2 months. After that Provence is gonna start to fade.

KATSUOBUSHI: What happens when you take a skipjack (aka bonito) tuna, cut out its loins, then smoke them and dry them and salt them and smoke them some more and maybe dry them a little further? Rock-hard bananas … at least that's what they look like. The stuff is so hard that you have to use a thing like a wood plane to cut it into thin shavings. Luckily you can buy it preshaved in bags that keep for approximately ever. Why keep it around? It's the basis of dashi, the cooking stock upon which Japanese cuisine floats. In that case the flakes are steeped and strained out, but you can also enjoy them sprinkled on everything from pasta to ice cream (seriously). Katsuobushi is also one of the weirdest foods in the world to watch. Finish the Grilled Shishitos (page 175) with them and behold what can only be described as a dance. The first time I witnessed this it scared the hell out of me.

LEAF LARD: Unlike most lard on the market, which is simply pig fat that's been hydrogenated to make it easy to work with and shelf stable (yuck), "leaf" lard is rendered from the soft fat that hails from around the kidneys. Its chemical makeup and crystalline structure differentiate it from other forms of lard and make it specifically well suited to pastry work, especially piecrusts. Its fats are less "saturated" than those in butter, so it's actually a healthier option; it doesn't taste at all porky, it's terrific for frying, and if refrigerated in a sealed jar, it keeps for months. My favorite application? The Little Brown Biscuits on page 17.

LIQUID SMOKE: I spent most of my life assuming this is terrible stuff, no doubt laden with artificial flavors and noxious chemicals, or worse, squeezed from wet cigarette butts or some such. Then I read that the "good stuff" contains nothing but smoke and water and is generated via a simple still. Intrigued, I made my own by placing a bag of ice on top of a metal bowl set upside down over a slightly larger tube cake pan perched atop a chiminea fireplace, inside which hardwood was smoldering. It took five hours to produce a couple of tablespoons, but, dang, was it tasty. Luckily there are a few brands out there still making it the right way, albeit faster than I can. Even if I didn't use it in food per se, I'd keep it around the bar to drip a drop at a time into my Smoky Tequila Sour (page 150).

MALDON SALT: There are two kinds of salt: salt you cook with and salt you finish with. Maldon salt's, large, gorgeous, light, and fluffy flakes melt in the mouth or crunch pleasantly on the tooth. It's harvested in Essex on the eastern coast of England and has been for a couple thousand years. Seawater is filtered and boiled and then slowly evaporated until the crystallization begins. Then the salt is raked, just so, to form the characteristic shape. I finish many dishes sweet and savory alike with Maldon, but the special cold smoked version tops my Butterscotch Puddin' (page 90). That's right ... butterscotch.

MEDJOOL DATES: Dates are the fruit of the date palm, and of the dozens if not hundreds of varieties, I think Medjool are the best. They have the largest meats and the sweetest flavor. I love dates, which makes it tough to explain why I never ever mentioned them for the entire 252 episodes of a food show I used to make. Doesn't matter. Medjool dates lend a rich, caramel goodness to stews, braises, and a host of appetizers and hors d'oeuvres that all depend on the date's signature stickiness to hold together. My favorite application is the Kick-in-the-Pants Smoothie on page 94 in which coffee, banana, and date come together to basically make the closest thing to a chocolate shake that isn't a chocolate shake. Despite their sweetness, dates are considered healthy due to their high vitamin content and because their sweetness doesn't seem to raise blood sugar. Store them in something airtight in the fridge for up to three months.

MUSCOVADO SUGAR: This very dark brown sugar is made in only two locations that I know of: the Philippines and the island of Mauritius, from whence my personal favorites hail. The difference between most commercial brown sugars and muscovado has to do with processing. Since granulated sugar is the sugar most people want and use, a great majority of sugarcane and beet sugar is refined to that level. The liquid left over from the process, molasses, is then added back as needed to make brown sugar. The makers of muscovado simply stop refining the sugar while it still has considerable molasses in it, which means it's less refined, and I think superior in flavor and texture. You'll pay more for it, but you'll get more flavor, and isn't that the point?

NUTMEG: Sumac may be my secret weapon, but I never go out without a nutmeg in my pocket, so it wins the spot on my culinary coat of arms. Although most folks associate nutmeg with holiday baking and, of course, eggnog, I don't carry it for those applications, though I do like eggnog quite a bit. And, I don't carry it because you can get high off it. You can, that is certain, due in large part to myristicin, a compound that breaks down in the liver into a "psychedelic" drug. It takes a lot to do the trick and there are lots of downsides, including possible death, so I'm not going to tell you how. What I like about nutmeg is that its flavor, though distinct, tends to cooperate with rather than dominate the foods with which it works. A little bit in béchamel defines that sauce. It elevates spinach and mushrooms and carrots, while still playing nice with the classic "pie spices," such as clove and cinnamon. I like it because it's a marble-size nut that's easy to carry and to grate. I also like that nutmeg often associates with booze, and not just eggnog. I've been known to grate it right into bourbon (especially if the bourbon is on the cheap side). If you don't believe me on all this, go make yourself a Mr. Crunchy (page 27) or an Oyster Po'boy (page 81) and get back to me. My one rule: *Always* grate it fresh.

In 1667 the English traded their last nutmeg-growing island in the Pacific to the Dutch in exchange for another island called Manhattan. #truestory

PEPITAS/GREEN PUMPKIN SEEDS:
Same thing, of course, they're just a lot more common in the cuisines of Latin America and as such are often available in the "ethnic" aisle under that name. Pepitas, Spanish for pumpkin seeds, are commonly used in Latin cuisines. Typically, pepitas are hulled and roasted or toasted prior to packaging.

QUINOA:
I have gone on record more than a few times over the last few decades saying that I deeply dislike quinoa. Again . . . superfood. But this time instead of the Aztecs or the Maya, it's the Incas who cultivated and cooked the seeds of the *Chenopodium quinoa* in the mountains of Peru as far back as 5,000 BCE. A member of the beet family, quinoa delivers an astounding amount of nutrition. There is quite a bit of protein containing nearly all the essential amino acids, anti-inflammatories, unsaturated fatty acids, and a whole bunch of phytochemicals, some of which are thought to reduce the chance for various cancers. So here again . . . we ought to be eating this stuff. But what I've come to appreciate is the flavor and texture, both of which are rather difficult to describe. What I do know is that this avowed quinoa hater always adds it to his oatmeal, and the Roasted Thanksgiving Salad on page 71 may just be my favorite recipe in this book.

PS: Many packagers mention rinsing quinoa prior to cooking, probably to ensure that any residue from the outer seed coat, which is quite bitter, has been removed. I only rinse my quinoa when I make a whole pot, but for small quantities I don't bother.

RED PEPPER FLAKES:
Few spice blends are looked further down upon. Maybe it's the pizzeria association or the fact that you never really know what you're going to get heat-wise. And that's pretty much true. Most jars of "red pepper flakes" contain crushed bits of at least four different chiles, depending on the heat level (according to the Scoville scale) desired by whomever is making the mix. Anywhere from 30,000 to 50,000 Scoville is the norm, so blenders will use whatever they need to get there. Then there's fruitiness and smokiness to be taken into account. I tend to reach for the flakes quite a bit (five or six recipes in this book call for them) and I have different brands I appreciate, but even they change with the seasons. That's why I've gotten to where I blend my own. But then, I'm a freak.

RICE STICK NOODLES:
Unlike wheat-based dry pastas, rice noodles can be hacked for a wide variety of textures simply by changing up how they're hydrated. You can simply soak them in hot water or you can soak them in lukewarm water. Or you can soak them, then quickly boil them. This means they lend themselves to everything from stir-fries to soups like the Pho Bo on page 11. Rice noodles can also be served cold in salads or on rolls, and since they're rice, there's no gluten to fret about.

SARDINES:
The word "sardine" refers to many varieties of small, oily fish in the herring family, and I heart them all, especially when they're in cans. I am, in fact, currently in possession of thirty-two cans of sardines from the United States, France, Portugal, and Spain. Unlike anchovies, I feature sardines front and center as evidenced by the dip/spread on page 168. Besides tasting great I have only one rule by the way: always oil, never water. Water-packed sardines actually taste worse than water-soaked tuna, and that's saying something. Did I mention that sardines are considered sustainable and deliver a heaping helping of omega fatty acids? Just sayin'.

In case you're wondering, "sprats" are the Baltic cousins of sardines and are traditionally smoked before canning. I have about twenty cans in stock, all from Latvia. Then there are kippers, which are herring that have been split, salted, then smoked. I have thirteen cans of those, and they're all from England.

SICHUAN PEPPERCORNS: First things first … this isn't pepper—that is *Piper nigrum.* The two are not even related. What we're talking about is the pericarp, or outer husk, of a variety of prickly ash. Although green specimens show themselves from time to time, here in the United States most of what we get are red. And we're lucky to get them at all, seeing as how they were banned for several years by the USDA for possibly carrying a disease called citrus canker, but now the supply is flowing once again. Sichuan peppercorns are the chief spice responsible for the characteristic flavor of Sichuan-style food; they are referred to as *ma la,* or "numbing spice." That's because Sichuan peppercorns deliver a citrusy, piney zing while putting the middle of your tongue to sleep. The first time this happens you may fear you are having some life-threatening allergic reaction. After you get used to the sensation it's quite pleasant … at least I think so.

SMOKED PAPRIKA: There are probably as many different types of paprika as there are varieties of *Capsicum annuum* growing around the world, and they deliver flavors ranging from sweet to semisweet to semihot and hot. The most famous hail from Hungary, where the chiles are allowed to slowly dry in the sun, but my favorites are from the La Vera region of Spain, where they dry their *pimentón* over smoldering fires. In any case, paprika loses its efficacy quickly, so purchase in small batches from reliable spice peddlers. Fun fact: Though considered critical to Spanish cuisine, *Capsicum annuum* is American in origin.

STAR ANISE: If making your own five-spice isn't enough reason to keep these pods around, you clearly haven't had the Thai Iced Tea on page 98 or the Pho Bo on page 11.

SUMAC: My secret weapon. I got into sumac when I was studying the history of hummus. Most of us learn to add lemon juice for acidity, but then I ran across some research suggesting that hummus was a standard in many parts of the Middle East long before citrus reached the area via the Indian subcontinent. What did they use instead? The crushed berries of a Mediterranean bush, not the poison sumac we grow in the States. Earthy yet lemony, unique yet oddly familiar, sumac is also a key ingredient in za'atar, which is kind of like the five spice of the Middle East. I tend to use it a lot on fried foods that can use some acidity to cut oiliness. Order from the Interwebs … I never see it in stores.

WHEAT BERRIES: Wheat gets a lot of bad press these days, what with all those empty calories and that (look away, children) gluten. But wheat berries, which aren't berries at all, are as whole as grains get and include the good stuff like the germ and bran. When cooked, they are nutty and pleasantly chewy and they play well with vegetables, herbs, and meats. It's worth pointing out that "bulgur" refers to wheat berries that have been parboiled, dried, and broken into pieces. That's not something you can easily do at home, but since I keep wheat berries around but not bulgur, when I prepare a bulgur recipe, I typically break the berries up in a food processor, use a bit more liquid, and alter the cooking time a bit. I always get away with it.

WHITE CORNMEAL: It's a Southern thing, and frankly I wouldn't even mention it here were it not for the fact that the country has been overrun by yellow cornmeal, which is a very different thing indeed. I suspect the culprit is polenta, the popular Italian dish prepared from coarse yellow cornmeal. I also blame all that yellow corn bread served at "Southern" restaurants. Truth is, Southern corn bread is not quite as lily white as a biscuit, but it's dang close, just as true grits (see page 18) are a heck of a lot paler than the aforementioned Italian porridge. Why this is important to me has to do with frying. Fine white cornmeal is absolutely superior to the yellow stuff when it comes to creating a fine, crisp, fried exterior on fried foods. Heck, I don't think I even have any yellow cornmeal.

DARK RUM

Mainly for cooking but for cocktails too. Myers's is the standard bearer and is typically blended from nine or so rums all distilled in pot stills so they've got a fair amount of complexity. To up the sweetness, some of the molasses these rums are distilled from are added back to the final product.

AMARO

If I had to enjoy but one category of spirit for the rest of my days it would be *digestifs*, specifically, amari (plural of amaro). Designed to aid digestion, an amaro is fairly high in alcohol and full of funky medicinal flavors. Amari are all bitter to some degree, but Amaro Montenegro, which is the most readily available brand in the United States, is a relatively mild place to start. Not bitter enough for you? Try Fernet Branca.

TEQUILA BLANCO

Although I prefer drinking mezcals, which are made from agave, but not only blue agave, which is the rule for tequila, I keep blanco, aka silver or plata, tequilas around for cocktails. They're straightforward and clean with none of the character of aged tequilas. The bottle pictured isn't a brand I'm big on, it's just what we had on hand and that's sorta the way I feel about blancos.

COCCHI ROSA AMERICANO APERITIVO

This apéritif is a blend of wines punched up with various fruits, herbs, and spices, including cinchona bark, whose quinine provides Cocchi's bark, so to speak. The white version is often used in a vesper in place of Kina Lillet, which was reformulated in the eighties. I prefer the red because it's fairly bitter but not nearly as bitter as Campari. (In case you haven't noticed, I've got a serious thing for bitter when it comes to beverages.)

BRANDY

Basically distilled wine or fermented fruit juice. There are hundreds of examples produced around the world, but I live in Georgia and we're the Peach State, so there. I use this in my sangria (see page 105), and nobody ever complains.

AND NOW FOR THE BAR...

A few of my favorite bar things. Spirits that I have on hand at all times and which are (mostly) used in the recipes herein.

CAMPARI

Hello, lover. This apéritif, whose bitterness is meant to stimulate appetite, is just the bomb. It's what makes a negroni a negroni and a boulevardier a boulevardier (a negroni with bourbon, basically) and that's good enough for me. Fruits, herbs, alcohol, water, and coloring. Originally the red came from carmine, made from crushed cochineal, a parasitic insect. Ah, those were the days. Pass the soda.

BOURBON

Look, we just don't have the time or space here to go wadin' into this pool. I have a lot of bourbon. Do you hear me? A lot. And yet, the one I reach for most often when mix-o-gizin' is this straight bourbon whiskey (aged at least two years, no added coloring or other . . . stuff) from the folks at Bulleit. That's not a paid endorsement, but if you guys want to talk, you can tweet me or call me or whatever.

BLENDED SCOTCH

American drinkers can go on and on about single malts, but when it comes to scotch for cocktails, I'm all about the blends. They're balanced and flavorful and not so darned expensive. I actually love the Johnnie Walker Blue but couldn't picture it because I was out . . . still am. Do you hear me, Johnnie!

LONDON GIN

Gin has had quite a renaissance of late, but this classic, still made in the heart of London, is what I reach for when a martini must be made. "Dry" means no sugar is added. Londons are typically around 90 proof and feature balanced, almost restrained botanicals with stronger hints of citrus. I keep mine in the freezer so that my martinis will require minimal ice.

APPLEJACK

The term "jack" used to refer to a process of freeze distillation that has pretty much been abandoned in modern times. This particular bottle contains apple brandy mixed with neutral spirits. It was made in New Jersey, a state that used to make so much applejack that the liquor was called Jersey Lightning. As far as I know, this is the last applejack made in the United States. I use it in cocktails (hot and cold) as well as meat glazes.

METHODS
(A FEW OF MY FAVORITE WAYS)

BREAD CRUMBS

I use bread crumbs quite a bit and I flat-out refuse to buy them. So, let's say you've got half of a baguette left over from dinner. You know that no matter what you do it's going to be stale by morning. That's because it's made from a lean dough and doesn't contain enough fat or sugar to hold on to any moisture. So tear it into 1-inch chunks. Place these on a pan and roast for 5 minutes at 300°F. Then remove the pan from the oven and pulse to coarse crumbs in a blender or food processor. Return the crumbs to the oven for another 5 minutes, or until just lightly browned. Cool thoroughly and seal in airtight containment for up to a month.

PREPPING A BUNDT OR TUBE PAN

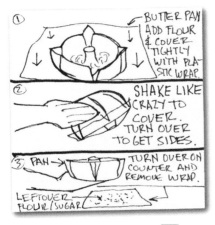

① BUTTER PAN, ADD FLOUR & COVER TIGHTLY WITH PLASTIC WRAP.

② SHAKE LIKE CRAZY TO COVER. TURN OVER TO GET SIDES.

③ PAN → TURN OVER ON COUNTER AND REMOVE WRAP.

LEFTOVER FLOUR/SUGAR

Freeing a cake from a pan with lots of nooks and crannies can be a pain, especially if the pan is older and has a fairly scratched-up surface. So, lube the pan lightly with shortening or butter (I prefer shortening as it doesn't con-tain water, which can complicate things), then dump in about 3 tablespoons of either flour or sugar, depending on what the recipe calls for, and cover with plastic wrap. Next, use a rubber band (like the ones they put around broccoli and asparagus) to secure the plastic around the pan's center tube before stretching the wrap around the outside of the pan. Now shake the heck out of it, turning it upside down several times to make sure the edges are coated. Remove the plastic and dump out the excess powder.

CHARCOAL PREP

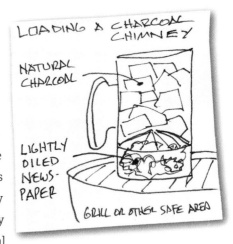

LOADING A CHARCOAL CHIMNEY

NATURAL CHARCOAL

LIGHTLY OILED NEWS-PAPER

GRILL OR OTHER SAFE AREA

All you need to buy is a chimney-style charcoal starter, which basically looks like a big metal tube with a well-insulated han-dle on it. You can buy one pretty much anywhere grills are sold. When you're ready to use it, fill the chimney with natural chunk charcoal (mine holds about 5 quarts), then lightly spritz a full page of newspaper with cooking oil or spray with nonstick cook-ing spray (about a 5-second blast should do it). Loosely wad the paper and place it in the bottom of the chimney, under the wire rack. Place this on your grill and light the paper. The oil will essentially turn the paper into an oil lamp that will burn about ten times longer than the paper alone, though I should point out that the nonstick cooking spray won't burn quite as long. Either fuel, however, will provide the charcoal with enough heat and time to kindle.

CLARIFIED BUTTER

This is one of my secret weapons. Not only does clarifying convert butter into a sauté-capable fat, the flavor is unlike anything, and I do mean anything, in the kitchen. Oh, and once the process is complete, the stuff will keep in a jar in the fridge for up to six months and up to a year in the freezer. That means you'll be able to make the crackers on page 170 any dang time you like. So, melt a pound of butter (that's four standard sticks) in a narrow, heavy saucepan over low heat until all the bubbles dissipate (that is, until the water has cooked out) and the liquid clears, 30 to 40 minutes. Strain through a fine-mesh strainer, being careful to leave any solids at the bottom of the pan. Always keep tightly covered as fat is notorious for absorbing flavors from both fridge and freezer.

FRY STATION SETUP

Remember, the food to be fried moves in this sequence:

I. Flour (to provide a kind of primer coat for the egg). Tap to remove excess (or egg will fall off).

II. Egg (for color and protein and adhesion of heavier crumb layer). Drain excess (or crust can fall off as much of the egg converts to steam during cooking).

III. Crumb coat (bread crumbs, cereal crumbs, stale doughnut crumbs, cracker crumbs . . . crumbs to provide flavor, color, and crunch).

IV. The fry pot (self-explanatory).

V. The drain rig (provides a place to cool and for excess oil to drain away).

If you want your fried foods extra crispy, try resting after the primary crumb coat, then re-egg and add a second crumb coat. I'd tell you to try a third, but that's just crazy.

COLD WATER PASTA METHOD

So, it turns out that despite what TV chefs have said in the past (including, me) dry pasta doesn't actually need a lot of water to cook, and that water doesn't have to be boiling when the pasta goes in. In fact, all you have to do is cover the noodles with cold water by, say, an inch (long strands will require a wide, shallow pot), bring the water to a boil, stirring often, then drop the heat and simmer for about 2 minutes. Not only is this faster, it wastes a lot less water and energy and I'm not sure that the quality of the pasta isn't actually better. Oh, and use a hand sieve or strainer to scoop the pasta out of the water rather than dumping the pasta into a colander. That starchy water is perfect for adjusting sauces.

SKINNING A MANGO

I say "skinning" because mangoes are like cats—there are a lot of ways to separate them from their . . . outer selves, so to speak. The fastest is to simply cut the two fleshy cheeks off the flat seed, then position skin up in the palm of your hand. Place the end over the edge of a drinking glass (see the sketch below) and push so that the skin goes over and

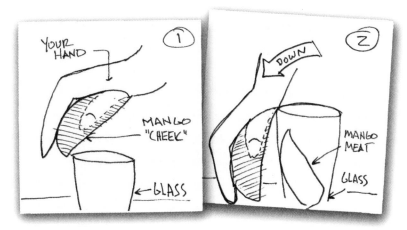

the flesh goes in. It's a great method if the mango is ripe, but since the glass isn't knife-sharp (unless you've got some really dangerous glasses), you tend to smush a good bit of the flesh. However, if you're blender bound, this is definitely the way to go. Otherwise, I go with the crosscut method: Remove the cheeks, hold the flesh up on a kitchen towel (for cut protection), and use a sharp paring knife to cut through the flesh in a grid pattern, without breaching the skin. Then, turn the cheek inside out and scoop off the squares with a spoon. This takes a little longer, but the yield will be neater and higher.

EVERYDAY CLEANING OF CAST IRON

Every time I cook in cast iron, I clean the vessel the same way:

1. Wipe it out.
2. Return it to medium to high heat.
3. Add 1 to 2 tablespoons oil.
4. Add 1 to 2 tablespoons kosher salt.
5. Wad up some paper towels and grab with tongs.
6. Scrub till the vessel is clean and the salt is dark brown/gray.
7. Dump out the salt.
8. Wipe with oil.
9. Cool.
10. Store.

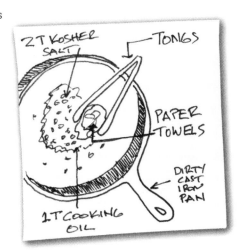

If the skillet is really hot and stuff is really stuck to the bottom (which isn't very often), I'll quickly deglaze it with water so that the goo boils off first. Then I dump the water and proceed with my normal MO.

FRENCHING

"Frenching" an onion (stop snickering) means to slice it radially from end to end. Think of it this way: Let's say you want to French a globe (seriously, enough with the snickering already). Start by halving it from pole to pole (1).

Next, lay it flat and cut along the lines of longitude from right to left (2). When you've sliced a quarter away, roll it over 90 degrees (3) and start again. You'll end up with a bunch of narrow wedges.

COOKING UNDER PRESSURE

Contrary to popular opinion, water does not boil (that is, convert from liquid to vapor) when it reaches 212°F. Simply put, it boils when the molecular energy inside the water surpasses the atmospheric pressure holding it in liquid form. We say that water boils at 212°F because that is what happens at sea level, aka "standard pressure," which is quantified by 29.92 inches of mercury (Hg) in a barometer, or 14.7 pounds of pressure per square inch (psi). This means that on an average day at the beach, you have 14.7 pounds of sky pushing on you from every direction. Now, if the atmospheric pressure decreases or the altitude increases, the boiling point drops, which is why water boils on Mount Everest at around 160°F. On the other hand, if you increase the pressure above 29.92 inches of mercury, the boiling point rises. And that's what a pressure cooker does.

Here's what happens:

- You load the pot with food and liquid.
- You lock the lid into place, which then seals the vessel via a silicone or rubber ring in the lid.
- You place the pressure cooker over heat and, depending on the make and model, the pressure inside rises to 10 to 15 pounds per square inch (20.36 to 30.54 inches Hg, respectively). A small hole fitted with either a spring-loaded or weighted valve allows

excess pressure to vent out. Typically, this creates a whistling sound, which lets you know that maximum pressure has been attained. At this point, the heat should be reduced until the cooker barely hisses.

- At 10 to 15 psi, the boiling point elevates to 237° to 250°F, cooking foods much faster than they would at 212°F. This is especially true regarding the conversion of connective tissues in meat to gelatin. This translates to saved time and energy.

Note: All modern pressure cookers have an emergency "burst disk" that will release the pressure should the primary become jammed or clogged. What's critical is that you don't fill the pot beyond the max-fill line, which should be clearly marked either on the inside or outside of the pot. Filling beyond this point will reduce the "head space" required for pressure to build.

Another note: I have two favorite brands—Kuhn Rikon and WMF. They're both pricey, but in this case, price really does reflect performance and durability.

One last note: Some pressure cookers are also pressure canners, meaning that jars of home-packed foods can be processed inside them for shelf stability. Those machines are more complex, and I don't recommend them for day-to-day cooking.

MORNING

Breakfast Carbonara

FEEDS 4 TO 6

The way I look at it, if you're going to eat pasta on a regular basis, you should probably have it for breakfast so you've got the whole day to work it off. With that in mind, I offer this riff on carbonara that delivers eggs, sausage, toast, and even a bit of citrus.

Now . . . where will I put that Nobel?

1 tablespoon grated orange zest

¼ cup fresh flat-leaf parsley leaves, finely chopped

¼ cup fresh bread crumbs

1 tablespoon kosher salt

8 ounces dry linguine, preferably whole wheat

8 ounces breakfast sausage

2 scallions, thinly sliced

4 large eggs, at room temperature

3 ounces finely grated Pecorino Romano

1 teaspoon freshly ground black pepper

1. Combine the orange zest, parsley and bread crumbs in a small bowl. Set aside.

2. Add 2 quarts water, the salt and linguine to a large sauté pan. Cover and bring to a boil over medium-high heat. Reduce the heat to low and cook for 4 minutes, or until the pasta is al dente. M

3. Meanwhile, cook the sausage in a 12-inch cast-iron skillet H over medium-high heat until brown. Add the scallions and cook until fragrant.

4. While the pasta and sausage are cooking, whisk together the eggs, Pecorino and pepper.

5. Drain the pasta, reserving ¼ cup of the starchy water. Add the pasta to the sausage, tossing the pasta to coat in the fat.

6. Remove from the heat, add the egg mixture, and thin as needed with additional pasta water.

7. Serve immediately with a generous sprinkle of the parsley mixture.

Always Perfect Oatmeal

FEEDS 2

If you think about it before going to bed, go ahead and put the water, oats and salt in the pot and let it sit overnight. The cooking will go even faster.

120 grams thick rolled oats (1 cup)
25 grams quinoa (unrinsed)
475 grams water (2 cups +
    2 tablespoons)
7 grams kosher salt

Combine, cover and place over low heat. After 15 minutes take a peek. If the water doesn't seem to be absorbing, re-cover, boost the heat a little and cook another 15 minutes. If at any time you see steam shooting out around from the lid, the heat's too high. Don't stir during cooking! If you want to add fruit, do so after cooking. Simply kill the heat, place the fruit on top of the oatmeal mixture, re-cover and wait 5 minutes.

Buttermilk Lassi

FEEDS 2

Although I've never personally been to the Indian subcontinent, I'm a huge fan of the various dairy-based beverages that go by the name "lassi." Most include yogurt and fruit of some type. My favorite home version is built instead on buttermilk, which I always seem to have left over from biscuit making, and mangoes, whose funky terpene flavors (kinda like pinesap) balance the b.milk's acidic snap.

12 ounces cubed mangoes
   (2 large specimens **M**)
2 cups buttermilk
1 tablespoon freshly grated ginger
½ teaspoon chile powder
½ teaspoon kosher salt

Combine the mangoes, buttermilk, ginger, chile powder and salt in a blender. Puree until smooth. Serve immediately.

4 frozen lassi cubes
½ ripe cantaloupe, cubed
1 peach, peeled and pitted, or
   1 cup frozen peach slices
½ cup plain low-fat yogurt
1-inch-long hunk fresh ginger
½ cup almond milk
½ teaspoon ground turmeric

Or ...

Freeze in ice cube trays **H** and use to make one of my favorite morning smoothies:

Place the lassi cubes, cantaloupe, peach, yogurt, ginger, almond milk, and turmeric in a blender. Blend until smooth, drink, and face a grateful planet.

Blueberry Pound Cake

MAKES 1 BUNDT CAKE, FEEDS 12

The best cakes are cakes that can arguably be served as breakfast, and this pound cake is a prime example. After all, it contains eggs and dairy and flour and fruit. Serve a thick slice, toasted golden brown, slathered with butter and sprinkled with sea salt, alongside a steamy cup of joe and go forth into your day knowing that no matter what else doesn't get done in your day, you got your cake in. Go you!

8 ounces (2 sticks) plus
  1 tablespoon unsalted butter,
  at room temperature

15 ounces plus 2 tablespoons sugar

15 ounces all-purpose flour

1 teaspoon baking powder

½ teaspoon kosher salt

4 large eggs, at room temperature

1 teaspoon vanilla extract

1 dry pint fresh blueberries (10 ounces
  or about 2 cups)

1. Heat the oven to 325°F. Coat a Bundt pan with 1 tablespoon of the butter and 2 tablespoons of the sugar **M**.

2. Cream the remaining 8 ounces butter and remaining 15 ounces sugar in a stand mixer fitted with the paddle attachment on medium for 5 minutes. Meanwhile, sift together 10 ounces of the flour, the baking powder and salt onto a paper plate **H**.

3. When the butter mixture is pale and fluffy, drop the mixer speed to low and add the eggs, one at a time, waiting for each to be incorporated before adding the next. Follow with the vanilla extract. Then slowly add the flour mixture.

4. Toss the blueberries with the remaining 5 ounces flour. Remove the mixing bowl and fold the berries and flour into the batter with a large rubber spatula. Pour the mixture into the prepared pan.

5. Bake for 75 minutes, or until an instant-read thermometer **H** registers 210°F. Cool in the pan on a cooling rack for 15 minutes before de-panning and cooling.

6. Serve with . . . your hands.

Pho Bo (Beef Pho)

FEEDS 4 TO 6

BEEF BROTH

1 cinnamon stick

6 whole cloves

2 pods star anise **P**

1 teaspoon whole fennel seed

2-ounce chunk fresh ginger, roughly
   crushed . . . don't bother peeling

1 onion, cut into thick slices

3 pounds mixed beef shanks and
   oxtails

1 pound chicken wings

½ large Fuji apple, don't bother peeling

5 teaspoons kosher salt

2 tablespoons fish sauce **P**

1 tablespoon palm sugar

TO SERVE

8 ounces eye of round, sirloin steak or
   London broil, thinly sliced

14 ounces thin rice noodles or "sticks"
   in the 1/16-inch range (banh pho **P**)

3 scallions, thinly sliced

2 Thai bird chiles, thinly sliced

1 cup bean sprouts

2 cups fresh herbs, including cilantro,
   Thai basil and mint

2 limes, quartered

SPECIAL EQUIPMENT

Pressure cooker **H M** , which you
should totally have anyway.

In the United States we have breakfast cereal. There are dozens of different types and styles and we all have our special ways of eating them. In Vietnam, they have pho. Pho equals breakfast cereal. Cook and eat accordingly.

Notice the broth calls for three cuts of beef. You can fudge a bit one way or the other, but I really think this combination makes for a superlative broth, and although the word "pho" actually refers to the rice noodles, the dish is really all about the broth.

1. In a large pressure cooker, toast the spices over medium-high heat until fragrant.

2. Add the ginger and onion and blacken slightly (some of the spices may burn a bit and that's just fine).

3. Add the meat and bones, wings, apple, salt and 10 cups of water. Apply the lid according to your cooker's instructions and bring to full pressure over medium heat. Once the cooker is steaming and whistling, back down on the heat to just maintain full pressure and cook for 30 minutes.

4. Meanwhile, place the eye of round in the freezer for 20 minutes to firm it up, then slice the meat very thinly across the grain. Cover and refrigerate while the broth continues to cook.

5. Remove the broth from the heat and allow to cool naturally for 5 minutes, then slowly remove the pressure.

6. Carefully remove the lid and fish out the meat, vegetables and spices from the broth. Save the shanks and oxtails for serving. Use a fine-mesh strainer to skim any small particles and/or scum from the broth. Stir in the fish sauce and palm sugar.

7. When they're cool enough to handle, slice the cooked shanks.

8. Everything above this line can be done up to a day ahead. When you're ready to eat, read on.

9. Soak the rice noodles in cold water for 30 minutes, then drain. Meanwhile, bring a large pot of water to a boil.

10. When you're really ready to serve, cook the noodles in the water for 10 to 15 seconds so that they are still a bit chewy. Drain thoroughly in a spider **H** .

11. Distribute the noodles into wide soup bowls (better be deep too) and top with the slices of (raw) eye of round and a few pieces of the cooked beef.

12. Cover with hot broth. Serve with the scallions, chiles, sprouts, herbs and limes and let diners garnish as desired.

Oatmeal Banana Bread

MAKES 1 LOAF, FEEDS 10

There are more than eight million recipes for banana bread on the Interwebs. Most of them are insipid and mushy. Due to the inclusion of toasted oats, this one is definitely not. And it's darned nutritious to boot.

168 grams old-fashioned rolled oats

84 grams all-purpose flour

6 grams baking soda

1 gram baking powder

¼ teaspoon kosher salt

112 grams unsalted butter, at room temperature

224 grams sugar

2 large eggs

½ teaspoon vanilla extract

238 grams mashed very ripe bananas (2 to 3 bananas)*

1. Heat the oven to 350°F.

2. Coat a 9 x 5-inch loaf pan with nonstick cooking spray and set aside.

3. Spread the oats in a thin layer on a half sheet pan and bake for 15 minutes, or until lightly toasted. Remove the pan and cool the oats for 2 to 3 minutes.

4. Grind the oats in a food processor until the consistency of whole wheat flour, about 3 minutes. Then pulse in the flour, baking soda, baking powder and salt.

5. Cream the butter and sugar in a stand mixer fitted with the paddle attachment on medium until pale and fluffy, about 3 minutes.

6. Drop the speed to low and add the eggs, one at a time, incorporating each fully before adding the next.**

7. Follow with the vanilla and bananas, and beat on medium-low until incorporated. The batter will look kind of curdled, but that's okay.

8. Add the flour mixture and beat on low speed just until combined.

9. Transfer the batter into the prepared pan and bake for 50 to 55 minutes, until the internal temperature reaches 200° to 210°F.

10. Cool the pan on a rack for 15 minutes before turning the loaf out and cooling completely.

* If your bananas aren't very ripe, roast them skin on in a 300°F oven for 40 minutes, until blackened and soft.

** Remember, a good batter is essentially an emulsion, so add those eggs slowly so that the water and fat phases have time to come together.

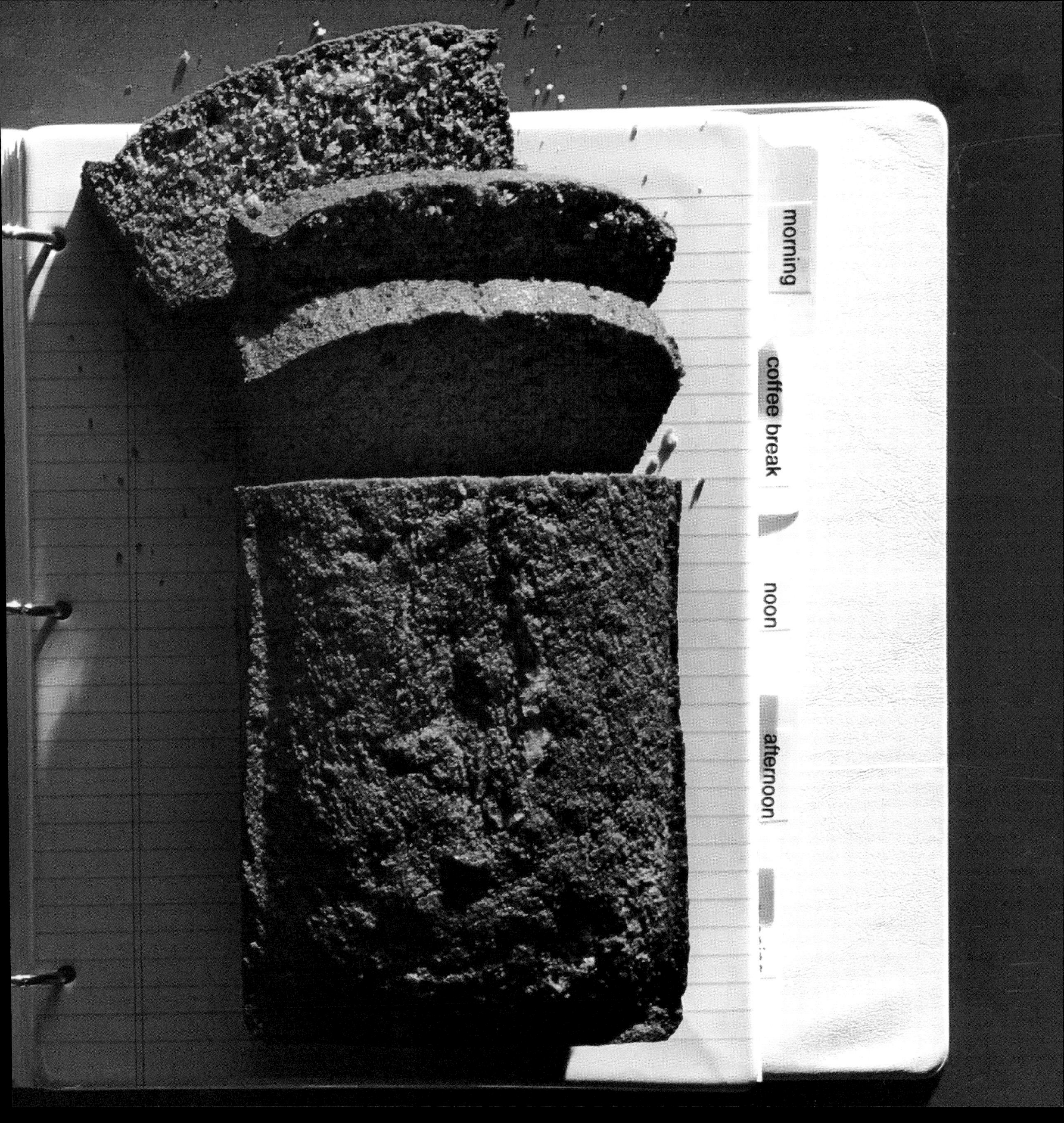
morning
coffee break
noon
afternoon

BCLT Tacos
(Blackened Catfish Lettuce Tomato)

FEEDS 4

It's generally accepted that the technique of "blackening" was created in the early eighties by Paul Prudhomme at Commander's Palace in New Orleans, and then perfected at K-Paul's. The concept is simple—apply a potent mixture of herbs and spices to fish and slap the fish on a very, very hot surface, then cook it very quickly. Blackened redfish became so popular at K-Paul's that it was often credited with nearly wiping out the redfish populations in the Gulf of Mexico. Personally, I vastly prefer blackened farm-raised catfish to redfish. Especially when it's in a taco.

CREMA*

1 cup sour cream
Zest of 1 lime
1 tablespoon fresh lime juice
1 garlic clove, minced
½ cup packed fresh basil
1 chipotle chile in adobo **P**

TACOS

4 teaspoons blackening powder **P**
1 pound farm-raised U.S. catfish
   (3 to 4 fillets)
8 corn tortillas
2 cups shredded romaine lettuce,
2 medium tomatoes, diced

1. To make the crema, combine the sour cream, lime zest, lime juice, garlic, basil and chipotle chile in a small food processor and process until smooth. Refrigerate until ready to use.

2. Sprinkle the blackening powder evenly onto the catfish fillets and set aside for 20 minutes.

3. To prepare the tacos, place a cast-iron skillet **H** **M** over high heat. When you think it's really hot, leave it for a few more minutes. If you turn the lights off and it glows . . . you're ready.

4. Add the catfish to the pan and cook until crisped and blackened, about 1 minute. Flip and cook another minute, then rest the fish on a plate off the heat for 1 minute. The fish should be opaque inside and flake easily when broken with a fork.

5. Turn the heat off and use the residual heat to warm the tortillas, or if you like a little more char, lay them, one at a time, right over gas burners set to low for about 30 seconds a side.

6. Break the cooked fish up into several pieces and serve inside the tortillas topped with the lettuce, tomatoes and crema mixture.

* A Mexican form of cultured sour cream, crema is closer in viscosity to crème fraîche. Purists will argue that using sour cream is cheating. I'm okay with that.

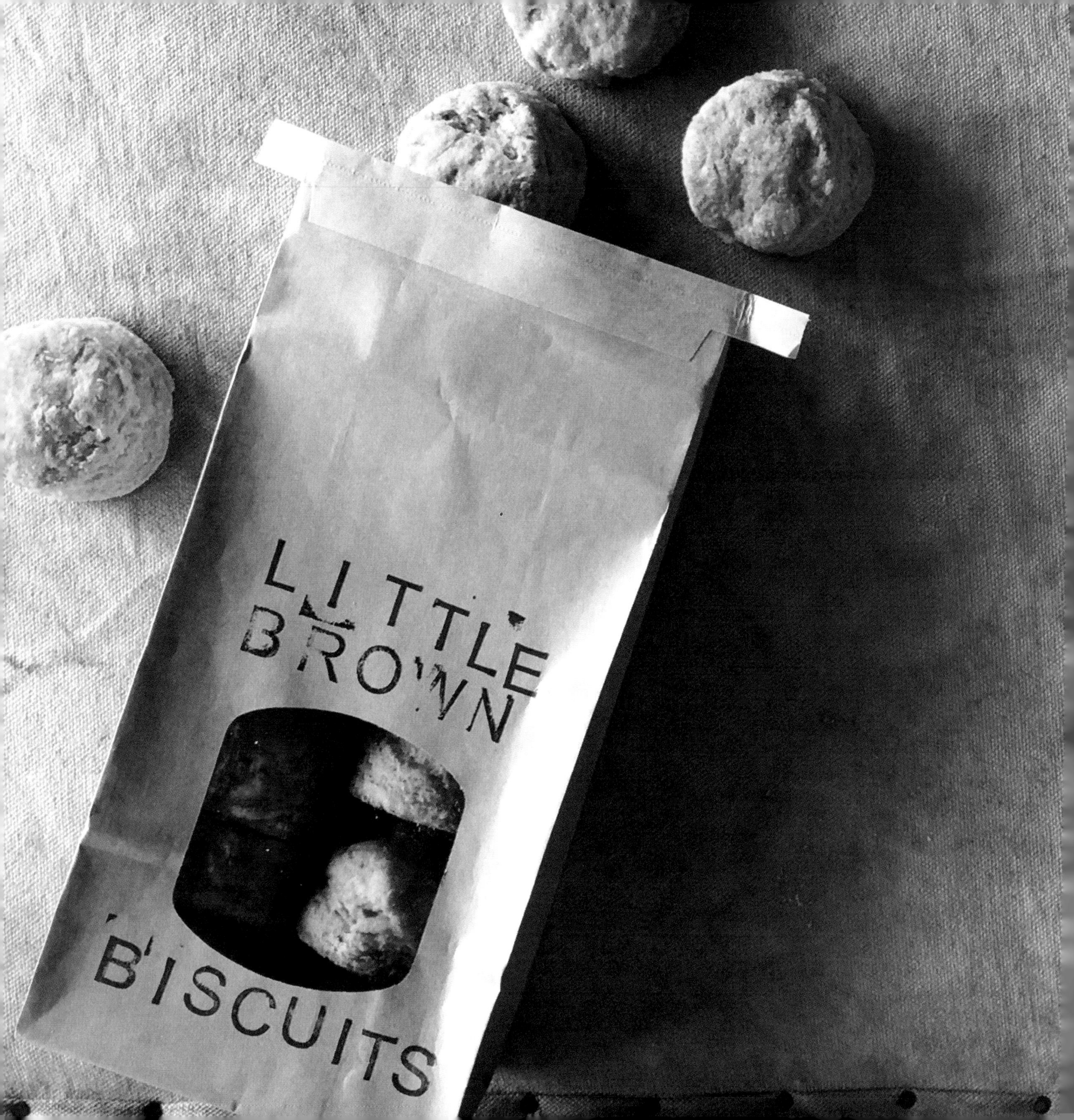
LITTLE
BROWN
BISCUITS

Little Brown Biscuits

MAKES FOURTEEN 2-INCH BISCUITS

2 ounces plus 1 teaspoon
nonhydrogenated leaf lard
5 ounces all-purpose flour plus more
for shaping
5 ounces whole wheat pastry flour
4 teaspoons baking powder
2 teaspoons kosher salt
1 cup cold buttermilk

Down South, biscuits are powerful symbols of culture as well as calling cards for cooks who know that regardless of what you've got in the pantry, technique holds sway. Now I'm not about to crown this my definitive biscuit—that's still somewhere out beyond the horizon—but this is now my go-to, everyday biscuit. The combo of AP and whole wheat pastry flour gives these biscuits both a tender texture and nutty flavor.

Though cold shortening or supermarket lard can be used, I prefer leaf lard. Leaf lard is the prime lard rendered from the abdominal fat around a pig's kidneys.

1. Heat the oven to 450°F. Coat a 9-inch straight-sided aluminum cake pan with 1 teaspoon of the lard.

2. Whisk the all-purpose flour, whole wheat pastry flour, baking powder and salt together in a large bowl. Quickly cut in the remaining 2 ounces lard until the mixture resembles coarse crumbs. Using a large wide spatula, stir in the buttermilk until the dough just comes together. The dough will be very loose and shaggy.

3. Dump the dough onto a lightly floured counter, fold it over onto itself 6 to 8 times, and pat into ½-inch thickness. Dip a 2-inch biscuit cutter or a 2-inch ring cutter **H** into the flour and cut out biscuits. Press the cutter straight down and do not twist! Place the biscuits in the prepared pan so they are just touching one another and the sides of the pan. Fold together the remaining dough and repeat cutting. Press down lightly into the center of each biscuit with a fingertip.

4. Set the pan on the middle rack of the oven and then boost the oven to 500°F. Bake for 12 to 14 minutes, until golden brown. Cool for 3 minutes in the pan before devouring.

Grits with Shrimp

FEEDS 4

2 pounds large, head-on, tail-on shrimp
(I prefer 31/35 count but 20/25 will
do too)*

6 cups water

1 tablespoon kosher salt

2 to 3 bay leaves

1 cup stone-ground grits (I prefer
Anson Mills)

1 tablespoon unsalted butter

1 tablespoon fresh lemon juice

2 teaspoons hot sauce

1 teaspoon Old Bay Seasoning

4 rashers bacon

4 scallions, finely chopped

Just like real Charlestonians during shrimp season, I consume this more at breakfast than dinner. If you want to follow suit, try soaking the grits overnight to shorten the cooking time. Oh, and since the grits are all too often neglected here, I put them first in the title.

1. Remove the heads and tails from the shrimp and save for making shrimp broth. Devein the shrimp and refrigerate while making the shrimp broth. Rinse the shrimp shells with cool water.

2. Heat a 4-quart pot over medium-high heat. Add the shrimp shells and cook until pink. Cover with the water and bring to a boil. Reduce the heat to a simmer and continue to cook, uncovered, for 45 minutes to an hour (looking for this to reduce to 1 quart). Strain the broth and cool over an ice bath.

3. Combine the cooled broth with the salt and bay leaves, whisking until the salt is dissolved. Set the grits in a 4-quart pot and top with the shrimp. Cover the grits and shrimp with the brine and stash in the fridge for at least 6 hours or overnight.

4. After the 6-hour brine: Remove any chaffs or hulls from the grits that may be floating on the surface. Remove the shrimp from the brine.

5. Bring the grits to a simmer over medium-high heat, whisking continuously until the grits boil, to avoid lumps. Reduce the heat and cook the grits for 30 to 35 minutes, until tender and creamy. Add the butter and stir to combine. Cover to keep warm while cooking the shrimp.

6. Toss the shrimp with the lemon juice, hot sauce and Old Bay. Set aside.

7. Cook the bacon in a large cast-iron skillet **H** **M** over medium-high heat until crisp. Remove from the pan to paper towels to drain. Add the shrimp and cook until pink, about 2 minutes per side. Coarsely chop the bacon, return it to the pan, and add the scallions. Stir to combine.

8. To serve, ladle the grits into a bowl and scatter the shrimp and bacon mixture over.

* I don't like to preach at folks about where they buy their groceries, but the U.S. has the best shrimp in the world, so stop buying those cheap "tiger" shrimp from China.

Chilaquiles!

FEEDS 4

2 tablespoons vegetable oil

6 medium corn tortillas, each torn into
4 to 6 pieces

12 ounces Roasted Chile Salsa
(page 176)

½ teaspoon kosher salt

4 large eggs

¼ cup crumbled cotija cheese

1 tablespoon chopped fresh cilantro

Like so many dishes of Mexican provenance, chilaquiles are sublime yet simple . . . little more than a stovetop casserole of tortillas and salsa. But simplicity isn't always "easy," and to pull it off you'll need a solid salsa (I always have my Roasted Chile Salsa on hand) and a good cast-iron skillet.

1. Place a rack about 6 inches under the broiler and heat your broiler to high.

2. Heat the vegetable oil over medium heat in a 10- to 12-inch cast-iron skillet **H M** until the oil barely shimmers. Add the tortilla pieces, a few at a time, to the pan. Once they're all in, they'll overlap, but move them around and flip them with tongs **H** every now and then and they'll fry evenly.

3. When the chips are crisp and slightly brown around the edges, ladle in the salsa and ¼ teaspoon of the salt. If you prefer your chilaquiles on the crunchy side, go with 9 ounces of the salsa; if you like them soft, as I do, go with 12.

4. Reduce the heat and allow the salsa to simmer and absorb into the chips a bit, 5 minutes. Since they're fried, the chips will hold together, forming layers.

5. Arrange the softened tortillas so that you can crack the eggs evenly across the surface, one in each quarter of the pan. Sprinkle with the remaining ¼ teaspoon salt.

6. Park the pan under the broiler for 3 minutes, or until the whites set. The yolks will (hopefully) still be a bit runny.

7. Remove the skillet and scatter the surface of the chilaquiles with the cheese and cilantro. Deliver to the table and serve right out of the skillet.

Overnight Coconut Oats

FEEDS 1

75 grams coconut milk

75 grams unsweetened almond milk

12 grams maple syrup

¼ teaspoon vanilla extract

40 grams old-fashioned rolled oats

30 grams dried fruit, such as
cranberries, cherries or blueberries.
No raisins please.

2 grams chia seeds **P**

3 grams flaxseed meal **P**

Pinch of kosher salt

Pinch of cinnamon

13 grams toasted coconut flakes

This is one of those dishes that is so nutritiously sound, it oughta taste terrible. But, alas . . . it's pretty damned fantastic. I have to give some credit to Yvonne, the craft services lady on *Cutthroat Kitchen*, though. She serves up a version of this every morning, with oats and coconut soaked in almond milk. I think she would have given me her recipe had I not driven a tank into her station. It's a long story.

1. In a 16-ounce jar, stir the coconut milk and almond milk together with the maple syrup and vanilla.

2. Weigh the oats, dried fruit, chia seeds, flaxseed meal, salt and cinnamon onto a paper plate **H**. Mix around with a fork, then fold the plate into a *U* and pour into the jar.

3. Apply the lid and shake to combine. Refrigerate overnight.

4. Serve right in the jar, topped with the toasted coconut.

Nitrous Pancakes

MAKES EIGHT 3-INCH PANCAKES, FEEDS 2

One day I was walking through the megamart, and there in the dairy section I spied a can of aerosol pancake mix . . . like Reddi-wip, but pancake mix. And I thought: GENIUS! And I took it home and cooked it and it was crap. But what an idea! Luckily, we have a nitrous oxide (N_2O) cream whipper in our possession. You'll notice that the ingredients below are in grams. That's because accuracy here really matters. So break out the digital scale **H**.

180 grams all-purpose flour

220 grams buttermilk

2 large eggs

52 grams sugar

1 tablespoon canola oil

1 tablespoon vanilla extract

¾ teaspoon kosher salt

1 tablespoon unsalted butter or, better, Clarified Butter **M**

SPECIAL EQUIPMENT

1 liter whipped cream siphon **H**

N_2O charger

Electric skillet

1. Whisk the flour, buttermilk, eggs, sugar, canola oil, vanilla and salt together and use a funnel to pour the mixture into the whipped cream siphon; do not fill above the maximum fill line. Lid the whipped cream siphon, charge with an N_2O charger and shake vertically 15 to 20 times. Set aside for 20 minutes.

2. Heat an electric skillet to 350°F. Melt a teaspoon of butter in the skillet. Invert the whipped cream siphon and (carefully) dispense a 3-inch round of batter for each pancake, keeping at least 2 inches open between them. Cook for 1 minute per side, or until golden brown. Repeat for the remaining batter.

3. I would tell you how to serve them, but you already know, don't you.

Mr. Crunchy

FEEDS 4

If you invert those two words of the title and translate to French, you get croque monsieur, one of the world's great sandwiches. If you've never had one, it's essentially a griddle ham sandwich, smeared in béchamel sauce and topped with a lot of Gruyère cheese, that is then broiled to golden brown, semi-crusty gooiness. Yeah . . . what could be wrong with that? Mr. Crunchy is packed with fat, so the way I figure it, you'd better make all those calories count by constructing this sandwich as painstakingly perfectly as possible. For me that means making your own herbes de Provence blend and taking great care with every step of the process. Your patience will indeed be rewarded.

BÉCHAMEL*

2 tablespoons (¼ stick) unsalted butter

1 ounce all-purpose flour

8 ounces whole milk

1 teaspoon fresh thyme leaves

½ teaspoon kosher salt

½ teaspoon ground white pepper

¼ teaspoon *freshly* grated nutmeg **P**

SANDWICHES

4 slices sourdough bread, cut ½ inch thick

1 tablespoon whole grain mustard

8 ounces thinly sliced black forest ham

8 ounces grated Gruyère cheese

2 teaspoons herbes de Provence blend **P**

1. Melt the butter in a small saucepan over medium heat. Whisk in the flour and cook for 2 minutes, whisking occasionally, until the roux smells nutty. Whisk in the milk, thyme, salt, white pepper and nutmeg. Cook the milk mixture, whisking to smooth, until thickened. Set the sauce aside to cool and thicken slightly more while preparing the sandwiches.

2. Set the top rack 6 inches under the broiler and heat the broiler to high. Line a half sheet pan with aluminum foil **H**, spray with a little nonstick cooking spray, and set the bread slices on the pan. Spread the mustard on the bread slices.

3. Top the bread slices with 2 ounces each of the ham. Cover the ham evenly with the béchamel and top each with 2 ounces Gruyère. Sprinkle each sandwich with ½ teaspoon herbes de Provence. Broil these open-face sandwiches for 2 to 3 minutes, or until the cheese is melted and lightly browned.

4. Serve with a knife and fork and plenty of napkins.

Note: If you add a fried egg to the top of the sandwich, it becomes a croque madame.

* About the Béchamel
One of the French "mother sauces," béchamel is essentially roux-thickened milk seasoned with white pepper and nutmeg. Without it, Mr. Crunchy just isn't a croque monsieur.

Scrambled Eggs V3.0

3 large eggs

1 teaspoon water

1 teaspoon mayonnaise[*]

½ teaspoon harissa paste

⅛ teaspoon kosher salt

1 teaspoon unsalted butter

SPECIAL EQUIPMENT

Well-cured cast-iron skillet **H** **M** in the 10- to 12-inch range

An infrared thermometer **H**[**]

Oh, and a basting brush of some type

Eggs never cease to amaze me. Whenever I grow weary of cooking, or of eating for that matter, eggs revive me. My favorite form to serve them: the humble scramble. I've filled an entire journal over the years as I've theorized and experimented with different hypotheses. But in the end, it's version 3.0 that I keep coming back to.

1. Place the skillet over medium heat and bring the surface temperature to 380°F. This should take 3 to 5 minutes. Why not high heat? Because you're more likely to shoot right through the target temperature, that's why.

2. Meanwhile, whisk together the eggs, water, mayonnaise, harissa and salt until a light and homogenized mixture is formed.

3. When the surface of the pan hits 380°F, turn off the heat and add the butter. Use the basting brush to push it around to quickly coat the entire bottom of the pan as the butter melts.

4. As soon as the butter melts, pour in the egg mixture and count to 10. Stir with a rubber spatula and count to 5. Stir again to get any remaining liquid down into the pan and count to 5.

5. Transfer the finished eggs to plates, and consume. Note, please, the silky texture and hint of spice.

Have a nice day.

[*] Since scrambled eggs are essentially an emulsion, I figure why not enhance their texture with another emulsion? The results are creamier than egg, or even egg and dairy alone, can produce. You'll never know the mayo is in there until you go and leave it out.

[**] Why? For this to work properly, you need an iron pan because the technique depends on high heat retention and a black surface. Why black? Because black surfaces give the most reliable results when you are measuring temperature with an infrared thermometer. If you don't have one, an infrared thermometer looks like a little ray gun and most do have lasers in them to tell you exactly where you're measuring. You pull the trigger and it reads the actual surface of the pan. You can order up a good specimen for around fifty dollars online. I'm particularly fond of those manufactured by ThermoWorks.

New Year's... Southern-Style

All good Southerners know that you best serve up a pot of greens and some black-eyed peas on New Year's Day else there won't be no cash money (that's the collards) and no coins (the peas) through the coming year. And, of course, corn bread means . . . corn bread.

THE GREENS
Makes about 2 quarts
4 bunches collard greens*
2 teaspoons kosher salt
2 teaspoons red pepper flakes P
¼ cup vegetable oil
¼ cup red wine vinegar
1 smoked ham hock

FOR THE GREENS

1. Fill your sink with cold water and tear the greens off the ribs. I usually get about 6 pieces off each leaf. Slosh the leaves around in the water to remove any dirt/bugs/et cetera and tear up the big pieces as you go. You don't cut collards with a knife . . . 'less you're a Yankee.

2. Put your pressure cooker H over high heat. Transfer enough greens to the cooker to fill it halfway. Don't drain or dry the leaves, as the water will become the cooking liquid and thus the pot liquor that embodies the soul of the dish. Cook the greens until they wilt and turn bright green, about 5 minutes. Remove to a large bowl and repeat with the remaining greens.

3. Move all of the greens back to the cooker and stir in the salt, red pepper flakes, vegetable oil and vinegar. Finally, nestle the ham hock within the greens. Affix the lid (check the manual). Once the cooker comes to pressure, releasing steam in a constant stream, reduce the heat to low and cook for 30 minutes, maintaining an even "hiss."

4. Kill the heat and release the pressure on the cooker. (Most modern cookers use a spring-loaded device or valve that will vent off the pressure.) If you don't want to wait, simply move to the sink and spray the lid and sides with cold water. Once the pressure lock is released, open the cooker and use tongs H to remove the greens to a bowl. Leave the hock and the liquid inside and reaffix the lid. Bring the cooker back to pressure over high heat, then reduce the heat to low and cook for another 30 minutes.

5. Release the pressure and open the cooker. At this point the hock will be very broken down and the liquid will be fragrant. Remove the hock and allow it to cool enough to peel off the outer layer of fat and pick the meat off the bone. Stir that and the greens back into the broth.

6. Serve, or cool and freeze.... Collards freeze well.

(continued on page 32)

* A bunch is typically 1½ to 2 pounds. So the four bunches called for here should fill a standard kitchen sink (21"x16"x7").

THE BLACK-EYED PEAS

Makes about 1 quart

20 ounces fresh (as in not dried) black-
  eyed peas

½ onion, chopped (5 ounces)

1 tablespoon kosher salt

1 tablespoon dried Italian herb mix

1 teaspoon freshly ground black
  pepper

1 tablespoon unsalted butter

THE CORN BREAD

Makes one 8-inch corn bread

Since this corn bread contains flour, it
would be considered "fancy" or "city"
corn bread.

1 cup white cornmeal P

1 cup all-purpose flour

¼ cup sugar

1 tablespoon baking powder

1 tablespoon kosher salt

2 large eggs

⅓ cup vegetable oil

1¼ cups buttermilk

FOR THE BLACK-EYED PEAS

1. Place the black-eyed peas in a saucepan
and add water to cover by 2 inches. Bring
to a boil over medium-high heat. A lot of
nasty foam will be created, so once the
water reaches a boil, remove the pan from
the heat and use a spoon to remove the
foam. Drain the peas in a colander and
rinse with cold water.

2. Return the peas to the pan and add
enough water to cover by 1 inch. Stir in the
onion, salt, herb mix, pepper and butter.
Bring to a boil over high heat, then reduce
the heat to maintain a bare simmer, stirring often until the beans are soft, 60 to
90 minutes.

3. Serve the peas in a small bowl with
plenty of the pot liquor.

FOR THE CORN BREAD

1. Heat the oven to 400°F. Lightly oil an
8-inch cast-iron skillet H M and place
in the oven to heat for at least 30 minutes.
If you overoil the pan, there will be some
smoke, but trust me, you want that
pan hot.

2. Whisk the cornmeal, flour, sugar, baking
powder and salt together in a large bowl.
Whisk the eggs, vegetable oil and buttermilk together in another bowl. Add the
egg mixture to the cornmeal mixture and
mix roughly together with a spatula. Carefully pour the batter into the hot skillet
and bake for 25 minutes, or until golden
brown and just set in the center.

3. Turn out the finished bread onto a cutting board and cool for 3 minutes before
cutting and serving with plenty of butter
(or, if you're hard core, crushed up in a
bowl of buttermilk).

4. Serve these three dishes together and
get ready to be all kinds of rich in the new
year. As for the beverage of choice: iced
sweet tea or beer. There isn't a wine that
goes with collards.

The Griswold Manufacturing Co. of
Erie, PA, made cast-iron for nearly
100 years. If you find any buy it
and send to me!

GRISWOLD No 8 OLD

COFFEE BREAK

Seedy Date Bars

MAKES TWELVE 1-1/2 X 4-INCH BARS

We all remember the line from *Raiders of the Lost Ark*, right? "Bad dates." Well, this date bar is never bad because it's pretty much a superfoods convention. In case you doubt, I've included a few nutritional attributes to the right.

1. Line an 8 x 8-inch pan with parchment paper.*

2. I have to warn you . . . things are going to be sticky. I usually spray the food processor work bowl and blade with a little nonstick cooking spray. Combine the dates, apricots, crystallized ginger, orange zest and salt in the bowl of a food processor and process for 1 minute, or until the mixture forms a thick paste, stopping to scrape down the sides of the bowl one time.

3. Heat a 12-inch skillet and cook the pepitas over medium-low heat, tossing occasionally, for 1½ minutes, then add the sunflower seeds and continue toasting for another 5 minutes. Finally, add the coconut, chia seeds, flaxseeds and sesame seeds and toast for 3 minutes, or until the mixture is fragrant and the sunflower seeds and coconut are lightly browned.

4. Add the toasted seed mixture to the sticky stuff in the food processor and pulse 8 times, 3 seconds a pulse.

5. Scrape the mixture into the prepared pan and press into an even layer with a rubber spatula. Refrigerate for 2 hours, then cut into 12 bars with a pizza cutter. Store, separated with parchment, in an airtight container for up to 1 week.

6. Consume as a breakfast or any time a quick energy boost is required.

* If you keep a spritz bottle of H$_2$O around, give the baking pan a squirt before you put in the parchment paper to help hold the paper in place.

8 ounces pitted Medjool dates P
FOR: fiber, potassium

4 ounces dried apricots
FOR: vitamins A and C

1 ounce crystallized ginger P
FOR: gingerol (anti-inflammatory)

1 tablespoon orange zest (from ½ orange)

½ teaspoon kosher salt

2 ounces pepitas/green pumpkin seeds P
FOR: magnesium, zinc

2½ ounces raw sunflower seeds
FOR: selenium, copper

¾ ounce unsweetened coconut flakes
FOR: vitamins A and E, polyphenols

2 tablespoons chia seeds P
FOR: omega-3 fatty acids, fiber

1 tablespoon whole flaxseeds P
FOR: omega-3s, manganese, vitamin B_1

1 tablespoon sesame seeds
FOR: various minerals

Cold Brew Coffee

SERVES 1

40 grams coarse-ground coffee*
100 grams boiling water
Pinch of kosher salt
200 grams ice
100 grams cold water

I consume ridiculous amounts of coffee, and most of the coffee I drink is cold and no, that doesn't mean I just brew a pot of coffee and chill it. To my taste, coffee that's to be served cold needs to be brewed specifically for that mission. I've played around with just about every variable you can imagine—method, ratio, grind, temperatures—and this is the combination that gets me where I need to go. And yes, you should weigh by grams.

1. Weigh the coffee into a pint-size glass jar.

2. Add the boiling water, stir, and cover loosely for 3 minutes.

3. Remove the lid and add the salt and ice, followed by the cold water.

4. Tightly fix the lid and refrigerate for 6 hours.

5. Strain through a paper coffee filter set inside a hand strainer. Add ice, and enjoy.

* I prefer a darker roast for this, and as you know, grinding to order is advised.

Peach "Cobbles"

4 pounds frozen sliced peaches

10 ounces granulated sugar

1 ounce (¼ stick) unsalted butter

1 tablespoon vanilla extract

14 ounces all-purpose flour, plus extra
for dusting

1 tablespoon baking powder

2 teaspoons kosher salt

1 cup buttermilk

1 cup plus 2 tablespoons heavy cream

2 tablespoons Demerara sugar **P**

That's right . . . frozen peaches. They're available everywhere, year-round, and I think they actually make a better dessert here because they break down more evenly as they cook. Thank all those little ice crystals.

If you don't have a 12-inch cast-iron skillet . . . get one. If you try to bake this in anything else, you'll be sorry.

Yes . . . you're making biscuits!

Demerara crystals are dry and large so that they remain crunchy even after baking.

Yes, this is a cobbler with an r, but when you see the finished dish, you'll totally get it.

1. Heat the oven to 375°F.

2. Combine the peaches, 8 ounces of the granulated sugar and the butter in a 12-inch cast-iron skillet **H** **M** over medium-high heat.   (The skillet will be very full.) Cook for 45 minutes, stirring regularly, until the peaches have reduced by half, are very tender and the liquid they've given up has thickened. Add the vanilla extract and cool slightly while you are preparing the dough.

3. Whisk together the flour, the remaining 2 ounces granulated sugar, the baking powder and salt in a large bowl. Add the buttermilk and stir to combine. Add 1 cup of the heavy cream and stir to create a moist but not sticky dough.

4. Dump the dough onto a lightly floured work surface. Gently press the disk out into a ¾-inch thickness. Fold the dough over onto itself 3 or 4 times and then gently pat it back out to a ¾-inch thickness. Use a pizza cutter to slice the dough into 1-inch squares.

5. Arrange the dough pieces on top of the peaches, so that they resemble cobblestones. Press the dough down into the peaches slightly. Brush the tops with the remaining 2 tablespoons cream and sprinkle generously with the Demerara sugar.

6. Bake for 20 to 25 minutes, until the peaches are bubbling and the biscuit topping is brown. Cool for 15 minutes before devouring.

7. Serve with ice cream or whipped cream, or just use your hands.

Amaranth Wafers

MAKES 36 COOKIES

WAFERS

100 grams whole amaranth P
195 grams dark brown sugar
55 grams unsalted butter,
   at room temperature
75 grams amaranth flour
3 grams dried orange peel
¼ teaspoon kosher salt
⅛ teaspoon baking powder
1 large egg
½ teaspoon vanilla extract
30 grams chopped Candied
   Orange Peel (recipe follows)

CANDIED ORANGE PEEL

Makes 1 cup
2 large oranges
2 cups sugar

FOR THE WAFERS

1. Heat an 8-inch nonstick skillet over medium-high heat for 2 minutes. Add about a tablespoon of the whole amaranth and shake into an even layer. Cover the pan and let the amaranth pop for 1 minute, or until the popping slows. Immediately remove to a bowl and continue popping the remaining amaranth a tablespoon at a time. When finished, allow to cool while you continue the batter.

2. Place the brown sugar and butter together in the work bowl of a stand mixer fitted with the paddle attachment and cream on medium speed for 2 minutes.

3. Meanwhile, whisk the amaranth flour, dried orange peel, salt and baking powder together and set aside.

4. Slow the mixer and beat in the egg and vanilla. Slowly add the flour mixture, followed by the popped amaranth and candied orange peel. Chill the batter for 30 minutes.

5. Heat the oven to 325°F.

6. Drop the batter by the tablespoonful onto parchment paper–lined half sheet pans, 12 to a pan. Bake for 10 to 12 minutes. Cool for 1 minute on the pans before moving to racks to cool completely. Sealed in an airtight vessel, the cookies will keep for 2 weeks. They freeze well too.

FOR THE CANDIED ORANGE PEEL

1. Quarter the oranges. Use a thin knife to remove the part you'd normally eat, which . . . you should eat. Then, remove as much of the white pith from the peel as possible. (This you should not eat.) Slice the orange peel into ¼-inch strips.

2. Move the strips to a medium pan, cover with water, and boil over medium-high heat for 15 minutes. Drain and rinse.

3. Back into the pan go the boiled orange peels along with the sugar and 2 cups water and cook for 45 minutes over medium-high heat. Lower the heat and cook for another 10 to 15 minutes, until the syrup reduces and dry sugar crystals begin to form. Immediately pour out the peels onto a cooling rack set over a piece of parchment. Spread the orange peel pieces into an even layer, allowing any excess sugar to fall away. Cool for 1 hour before storing. Oh, and keep any stray sugar—it's excellent for sweetening tea.

Lacquered Bacon

FEEDS 4 TO 6, OR MAYBE JUST 1

Because you should be able to have your bacon and your candy too.

1 pound thick-cut bacon

½ teaspoon coarsely ground black pepper

7 tablespoons dark muscovado sugar P

¼ teaspoon red pepper flakes P (or more if you're up to it)

1. Heat the oven to 400°F. Line a half sheet pan with parchment paper and set a cooling rack inside the pan.

2. Lay the bacon on the rack in a single layer so that there's little or no space between the pieces.

3. Liberally sprinkle one side of the bacon slices with ¼ teaspoon of the black pepper, 4 tablespoons of the sugar and the red pepper flakes.

4. Set the sheet pan in the oven and roast the bacon for 15 minutes. Remove the pan and use the back of a spoon to spread the dissolved sugar-pepper mixture evenly across the slices of bacon. Wait for 1 minute.

5. Flip the bacon over and liberally sprinkle the other side of the bacon with the remaining ¼ teaspoon black pepper and remaining 3 tablespoons sugar.

6. Return the sheet pan to the oven and roast until the desired doneness: 15 minutes for chewy, 18 minutes for crisp. Cool completely before devouring.

Note: I like to serve the rashers upright in a Mason jar like piggy candy canes, which are pretty much what they are. Can be stored at room temperature for up to 1 month if tightly sealed in a zip-top bag.

Apple Spice Bundt Cake
with Rum Glaze

MAKES 1 BUNDT CAKE AND 2 CUPS GLAZE, FEEDS 12

This cake is produced via the "creaming method," which follows a very simple order of four operations:

1. Cream together fats and sugars.
2. Slowly mix in eggs and liquids.
3. Slowly add dry ingredients.
4. Fold in "Bits and Pieces."

Once you've got this down, you can produce approximately 73 percent of the cakes in the known universe.

CAKE

2 medium Granny Smith apples (224 grams each)

434 grams all-purpose flour

6 grams baking soda

8 grams ground grains of paradise P

1 gram ground nutmeg P

1 gram ground ginger

1 gram ground cardamom

1 gram ground allspice

½ teaspoon ground rosemary

⅛ teaspoon ground star anise P

3 grams kosher salt

336 grams unsalted butter, at room temperature

224 grams granulated sugar

196 grams light brown sugar

3 large eggs, at room temperature

1 teaspoon vanilla extract

100 grams pecans, chopped

100 grams crystallized ginger P, finely chopped

GLAZE

336 grams powdered sugar

14 grams rum B

¼ teaspoon kosher salt

28 grams Demerara sugar P

1. Set a rack in the middle of the oven and heat the oven to 325°F. Lightly butter a Bundt pan and dust with flour, tapping out the excess M.

2. Chop one of the apples into ¼-inch dice, leaving the peel on. Grate the other apple on the large holes of a box grater. Set both aside.

3. Combine the flour, baking soda, grains of paradise, nutmeg, ground ginger, cardamom, allspice, rosemary, star anise and salt in a large bowl.

4. Install the paddle attachment on a stand mixer and cream together the butter, granulated sugar and brown sugar at medium-high speed until fluffy and pale.

5. Reduce the speed to low and add the eggs, one at a time, mixing thoroughly after each addition, followed by the vanilla.

6. Add the flour mixture in three batches.*

7. Add the apples, pecans and crystallized ginger.

8. Transfer the batter to the prepared Bundt pan and bake for 75 minutes, rotating the pan after 30 minutes. Cover the cake during the last 15 minutes of baking if the top gets too brown. The cake is done when it pulls away from the sides of the pan, springs back when pressed or the internal temperature reaches 205°F.

9. Cool the cake in the pan on a rack for 30 minutes. Invert and remove the cake from the pan. Cool completely on the rack before glazing.

FOR THE GLAZE

1. Combine the powdered sugar, rum, salt and 28 grams water in a small mixing bowl. Whisk with a fork until smooth.

2. Drizzle the glaze onto the Bundt cake. Sprinkle with the Demerara sugar.

3. Allow the glaze to set for 30 minutes before serving.

* I always do this by sifting the flour mixture onto a paper plate H, which I then gently fold like a taco to feed into the mixer.

NOON

No-Can Tomato Soup

2 small red onions, chopped

4 large garlic cloves, smashed

6 tablespoons olive oil

2 28-ounce cans diced tomatoes

1 cup fresh orange juice

2 teaspoons kosher salt

½ teaspoon ground cinnamon*

2 teaspoons sherry vinegar

SPECIAL EQUIPMENT

Pressure cooker H

Yes, I too have fond flavor memories of the soup that Andy Warhol made famous. But now I have a soup can of my own called the pressure cooker, which can make soup just about as fast as a can opener.

1. Sweat the red onions and garlic in 3 tablespoons of the olive oil in a pressure cooker over medium-low heat until translucent.

2. Add the tomatoes, orange juice, salt and cinnamon and affix the lid (according, of course, to the manufacturer's instructions). Increase the heat to high. Once the cooker comes to pressure (a constant, loud hissing or even whistling will alert you), reduce the heat to low and maintain an even, low "hiss" for 6 minutes.

3. Kill the heat and release the pressure on the cooker (see M for a few notes on relieving pressure).

4. Remove the lid and add the sherry vinegar.** Puree with an immersion blender while adding tablespoons of the remaining olive oil in a steady stream.

Freeze the extra in a zip-top bag; laying the bag flat to freeze saves space *and* leads to faster thawing.

* The cinnamon brings more aromatics to the party than spice—trust me on this one.

** Because acidic flavors tend to get the smack-down from pressure cooking, I typically add vinegars, citrus juice and such after the fact. So why add the orange juice earlier? Because I'm more after sweetness and fruitiness than citric acid, that's why.

Grilled Cheese Grilled Sandwich

FEEDS 2

1 ounce (¼ stick) unsalted butter, at room temperature

4 hearty country bread slices, about ⅓ inch thick

3 ounces grated extra sharp Cheddar cheese (Cabot is my go-to)

3 ounces grated Gruyère cheese

1 teaspoon dry mustard powder

½ teaspoon smoked paprika **P**

¼ teaspoon freshly ground black pepper

SPECIAL EQUIPMENT

You'll need a charcoal starter **M**, a grill, a spritz bottle of vegetable oil and two grill spatulas, which, let's face it, you should have anyway.

＊ The oil will considerably extend the burn time of the paper . . . kind of like the oil in a lantern.

99.997 percent of the world's grilled cheese sandwich recipes flat-out lie. Why? Because they're *griddled* rather than "grilled." Well, the lies die right here, people. Not only is this sandwich cooked on a grill, the cheese that goes in it is cooked on a grill. It's double freakin' grilled! (Drops spatula, walks out.)

1. Spritz a couple pieces of newspaper with vegetable oil, wad them loosely, and stick them into the bottom of a charcoal chimney starter.＊ Fill the chimney with 2 to 3 pounds of natural chunk charcoal and set on the charcoal grate of a kettle grill. Light the paper and allow it to burn for 15 to 20 minutes, until the charcoal is hot and ashy. (If you hold your hand 6 inches over the chimney and it bursts into flames, you'll know the fire is hot enough.)

2. Meanwhile, butter both sides of the bread. Combine the Cheddar, Gruyère, mustard, paprika and pepper in a small bowl.

3. Fold a 24-inch-long piece of heavy-duty aluminum foil **H** in half, short end to short end. Set a large metal griddle spatula in the center and fold the sides up around the spatula, forming a tray. Spritz the spatula tray with a small amount of vegetable oil, then repeat with the second spatula.

4. Divide the cheese mixture evenly between the spatula trays and set aside. Set aside two additional 15-inch sheets of heavy-duty aluminum foil.

5. Carefully distribute the hot charcoal onto one side of the charcoal grate. Set the cooking grate in place and heat for 2 to 3 minutes.

6. Set the cheese-filled spatula trays on the grill over indirect heat. Cook for 6 to 9 minutes, until the cheese melts and bubbles around the edges. You may have to adjust the placement of the spatula trays to ensure even melting and keep the cheese from overheating and breaking.

7. Grill the bread for 1 to 2 minutes per side over direct heat.

8. Place 1 slice of bread on each of the reserved sheets of aluminum foil. Use a pair of tongs **H** to open up the end of the foil on one spatula, pour off any accumulated fat, and then slide the cheese onto 1 slice of bread. Top with a second slice, then fold the foil around the sandwich.

9. Repeat with the remaining cheese and bread and return the sandwich packets to the grill over indirect heat for 1 to 2 minutes.

10. Unwrap and savor slowly. Now that's a GRILLED cheese sandwich.

BBQ Potato Chips

FEEDS 4

1 tablespoon smoked paprika **P**

1 tablespoon dark brown sugar

1 teaspoon onion powder

1 teaspoon kosher salt

½ teaspoon chili powder***

½ teaspoon garlic powder

1 pound russet potatoes (4 medium), scrubbed and rinsed

2 quarts peanut oil

SPECIAL EQUIPMENT

Heavy pot

Collapsible steamer basket or Steel Lotus **H**

1 cup hardwood chips

For years I've been trying to make BBQ chips that are as good as what you can get in a bag. The trick? Smoke the potatoes. If you don't have an honest-to-goodness exhaust hood, you should either do this outdoors (I keep a butane cooktop on hand for just such occasions) or pull the battery out of your smoke detector.*

1. Soak 1 cup wood chips in water for 30 minutes.

2. Combine the paprika, brown sugar, onion powder, salt, chili powder and garlic powder in a food processor or a small coffee grinder reserved for spices. Pulse to a uniform powder. Set aside.

3. Slice the potatoes into ⅛-inch-thick rounds using a mandoline **H** or other slicer. Place half of the potatoes in a steamer basket.

4. Line an 8-quart stockpot (tall and narrow) with heavy-duty aluminum foil **H** and set the drained wood chips in the bottom. Set the collapsible steamer basket in the pot above the wooden chips, cover and set over high heat. "Smoke" the potato slices for 10 minutes (you may want to turn on your fan or hood vent), then remove the pot from the heat and let rest, covered, while you prepare the oil.

5. Heat the peanut oil in a 4-quart cast-iron Dutch oven **H** **M** over medium-high heat, to 325°F.

6. While the oil heats, line a large mixing bowl with paper towels.

7. Carefully add the potato slices, one at a time, to the hot oil. Using a spider **H**, constantly move the slices in the hot oil for 3 to 4 minutes, until golden brown and crisp. Remove the chips with the spider and hold over the oil to drain as much excess oil as possible.

8. Move the finished chips to the lined bowl and shake to remove additional oil. Adjust the heat as necessary to maintain 325°F and continue frying the potatoes in small batches.

9. When the final batch has finished frying, move the chips to a large brown paper bag. Sprinkle the chips with the spice mixture, fold the top of the bag over to seal and shake. Serve immediately.

* My smoke alarm is really hard to disable, so I tend to cover it with foil when I know I'm going to smoke up the place. (But I always leave a note on the counter to remind me to take it off.)

** "Chile" powder and "chili" powder aren't quite the same. Chile powder is nothing but ground chile peppers. "Chili" powder, which is meant for use in chili (the dish) is typically composed of "chile" powder and spices such as cumin, black pepper and salt.

My Big Fat Greek Chicken Salad

FEEDS 4 TO 6

This is my favorite use of leftover grilled chicken, or my One Pot Chicken (page 134), though in a pinch a store-bought rotisserie bird will do. And I should add, this dish is just as good with turkey. But I wasn't sure about mixing Greece and Turkey in the same title since they don't always get along.

½ cup plain Greek yogurt (either whole or low-fat works here)

2 tablespoons fresh lemon juice

2 tablespoons chopped fresh flat-leaf parsley

½ teaspoon kosher salt

Freshly ground black pepper

1 pound cooked chicken breasts or thighs, torn and roughly chopped

1 small cucumber, peeled, seeded, and chopped

1 Roma tomato, chopped

½ small red onion, finely chopped

½ cup crumbled feta cheese

¼ cup pitted kalamata olives, roughly chopped

1. Whisk the yogurt, lemon juice, parsley, salt and pepper to taste together in a medium bowl. Add the chicken, cucumber, tomato, red onion, feta and olives and stir.

2. Refrigerate for at least 1 hour before serving nestled down in a warm pita. Will keep, covered, in the fridge for 3 days.

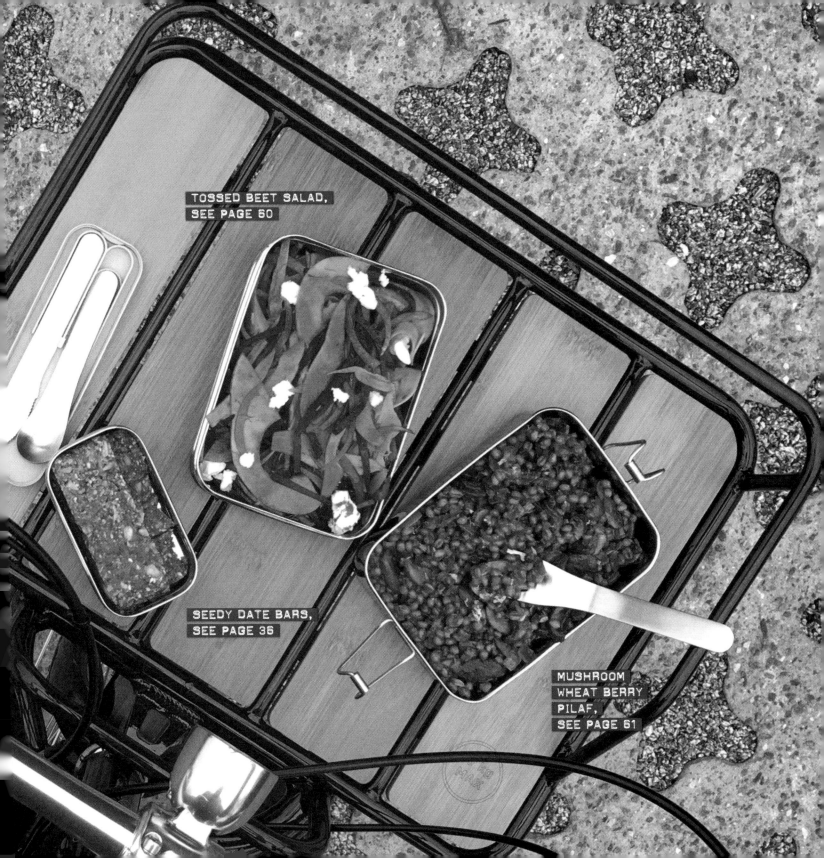

TOSSED BEET SALAD,
SEE PAGE 60

SEEDY DATE BARS,
SEE PAGE 36

MUSHROOM
WHEAT BERRY
PILAF,
SEE PAGE 61

Tossed Beet Salad

FEEDS 6

VINAIGRETTE

¼ cup dry red wine vinegar

2 tablespoons fresh lemon juice

2 tablespoons honey

½ teaspoon freshly ground
    black pepper

¼ teaspoon kosher salt

¼ cup olive oil

SALAD

1 small red onion, thinly sliced

1 large head fennel, cored, halved and
    sliced wafer thin (say, 3 millimeters)

1 Asian pear, halved, cored and sliced
    wafer thin

1 large jicama, peeled and cut into
    matchsticks

2 large beets, cooked,* peeled
    and cut into matchsticks

6 ounces goat cheese, crumbled

I remember sitting around the kiddie table at Thanksgiving and listening to my cousins griping about how gross beets were. One year we actually revolted en masse, refusing to so much as touch the plate of pickled spheres placed in the center of our table. Held sway by the bonding power of food, I went along. Later, I volunteered to clear the table, absconded with said dish, and ate the entire thing in the shower of my aunt's guest bathroom, the chintz curtain concealing my shame like the screen of a confessional. I don't hide anymore. And, I don't really talk to those cousins anymore, now that I think of it.

Note: As much as I love beets, there's no way I'd make this without a fixed-blade slicer or mandoline **H**. All of the slicing and dicing for this salad can be done efficiently on a mandoline or other fixed-blade slicer. If it were me, I'd start by thinly slicing the onion, fennel and pear, then add the mandoline's matchstick blade and slice the jicama followed by the roasted beets.

1. To make the vinaigrette, whisk the vinegar, lemon juice, honey, pepper and salt together in a large bowl. Keep whisking and slowly drizzle in the olive oil so that the mixture emulsifies.

2. To prepare the salad, add the red onion and fennel to the bowl and toss to combine.

3. Add the pear and jicama, toss to coat and set aside for 10 minutes.

4. Finally, add the beets and goat cheese and gently toss before serving.

* To oven-steam the beets, wrap them in a pouch of heavy-duty aluminum foil **H** and bake in a 400°F oven until tender, about 40 minutes.

Mushroom Wheat Berry Pilaf

FEEDS 6 AS A SIDE DISH OR 2 TO 3 AS A MAIN

1 cup wheat berries **P**

1 teaspoon kosher salt, plus more
    for seasoning

2 teaspoons olive oil

1½ cups chopped onions

5 large garlic cloves, minced

1 tablespoon unsalted butter

1 pound mushrooms, sliced*

1 tablespoon soy sauce

¼ cup dry red wine blend

¼ cup chicken broth

½ teaspoon fresh thyme leaves,
    chopped

1 teaspoon fresh rosemary leaves,
    chopped

1 teaspoon lemon zest, finely chopped

SPECIAL EQUIPMENT

Pressure cooker **H**

Whole wheat kernels, or wheat "berries," are as whole grain as whole grain gets. This is wheat with all the great stuff that we generally strip away during processing intact. Cooking pilaf-style brings out the grains' nutty flavor and chewy texture . . . and I mean chewy in the best possible way. The key is either very slow cooking or . . . a pressure cooker, my very favorite culinary time machine.

1. Toast the wheat berries in a dry heavy skillet over medium-high heat for 5 to 6 minutes, until the berries smell nutty. Keep them moving as they cook.

2. Transfer the toasted berries into your pressure cooker, add 3 cups water and the salt, attach the lid and put over high heat until the hissing begins and the pressure indicator rises.

3. Lower the heat to maintain a low hiss and full pressure, and cook for 45 minutes. Release the pressure using the manufacturer's instructions (or by running the pressure cooker under cool water for a couple of minutes). The berries should have a toothy texture. Drain excess water, if necessary. This can be done several days ahead of time and the berries kept in the refrigerator. Just bring them to room temp to complete the dish.

4. To prepare the pilaf, heat the olive oil in a large sauté pan over low heat. Add the onions and a pinch of salt and sweat until soft, about 10 minutes.

5. Add the garlic and continue cooking for 5 minutes.

6. Add the butter to the pan and melt. Then add the mushrooms and soy sauce. Increase the heat to medium and continue cooking for 5 to 10 minutes, until the mushrooms release their liquid.

7. Add the red wine and chicken broth and simmer for 5 minutes.

8. Add the wheat berries, thyme, rosemary and lemon zest and heat through. Adjust salt to taste.

* This is open-ended because so many different fungi can be used. I've made this with just about everything short of enoki, which would be creepy. As a default, brown cremini do just fine.

Turkey Sliders

1 tablespoon olive oil

2 large portobello mushrooms, stems and gills removed, finely chopped

½ teaspoon kosher salt

1 pound dark turkey meat, ground

2 tablespoons finely grated Parmesan cheese

1 tablespoon brown miso paste, at room temperature

1 dozen dinner rolls, sliced

Savory Greek Yogurt Dip (page 100)

Lettuce

Tomato slices

Turkey is probably the most American of meats, but when it comes to that most American sandwich, the burger, beef trumps turkey due to the presence of *umami*, the flavor associated with glutamic acid. By adding three umami-centric ingredients—Parmesan cheese, mushrooms, and miso—you can make ground turkey into a burger you'll actually want to eat.*

1. Heat a 10-inch cast-iron skillet **H** **M** over high heat, then add the olive oil, mushrooms and salt. Sauté for 5 minutes, or until the mushrooms are soft and golden. Remove from the heat and let cool.

2. Thoroughly combine the turkey, Parmesan, miso and cooled mushrooms using a potato masher or, better yet, your fingers. Divide the mixture into balls a little bigger than the size of a ping-pong ball. Cover and refrigerate for at least 30 minutes.

3. Return the skillet to medium heat. Flatten the turkey balls so that they're quite thin, about 2½ inches in diameter. Arrange the patties in the skillet, making sure they aren't touching. Cook for 2 minutes, or until browned, then flip and cook for another 2 minutes. Flip again for 1 minute and one final time for 1 minute, for a total of 6 minutes of cooking time.

4. Transfer the patties to a platter. Place the buns, cut-side down, in the skillet. Cover and cook for 2 minutes, or until brown. Dress a bun bottom with the Savory Greek Yogurt Dip; top with a patty, then lettuce, a tomato slice and a bun top.

---

* There's been a considerable amount of debate over the last few years questioning whether or not turkey is actually better for you than beef from both calorie and fat composition standpoints. My reason for including this recipe has nothing to do with health. I just like ground turkey. And considering the amount of beef Americans consume, I don't see anything wrong with mixing up my meaty menu a bit.

Beale Street Cheeseburger

MAKES 4 CHEESEBURGERS

2 quarts peanut oil, for frying . . .
  Yeah, what I said . . . frying.

12 ounces ground beef

1¼ ounces grated Cheddar cheese

1 teaspoon smoked paprika P

1 teaspoon garlic powder

Mayo and mustard

4 hamburger buns or (soft) kaiser rolls, split

12 to 15 dill pickle slices or "chips"

While touring with my road show I spent a day chowing in Memphis. Everyone urged me to try the burger at Dyer's on Beale Street, where they don't grill their burgers. They deep fry them in a grease that supposedly hasn't been changed since they opened. You watch the burger being fried and think it'll be a "one bite then good-bye" taste. Then, you try a bite. Here's my take.

Believe it or not, as long as you keep the oil between 300° and 325°F, this will be the most un-greasy burger you've ever enjoyed.

1. Get a nice big Dutch oven and add enough peanut oil or shortening to be 2 inches deep. Install your candy/fry thermometer **H** to the side of the pot and crank the heat to medium-high. Your thermal destination is 320°F (see Fry Station Setup **M**).

2. Place an oven rack in the top position and heat your broiler. This is a perfect time to use your toaster oven if you have one.

Meanwhile...

3. Weigh out the meat into four 3-ounce portions. Roll into balls and set aside. Do not refrigerate.

4. Grate the Cheddar. Toss the grated cheese with the paprika and garlic powder until all the powder has stuck to the cheese.

5. Place a thin layer of mayo on the bottom half of the buns. Place half of the cheese mixture on top of this. Spread mustard on the bun tops and place the rest of the cheese on this. So you have half the cheese on the bottoms (on mayo) and half on the tops (on mustard). Place these under the broiler so that the cheese melts as you cook the burgers.

6. When the oil hits 320°F, place one of the meat balls on an upside-down sheet pan. Dip a wide metal grill spatula into the hot fat, then use it to smash and spread the meat ball out into a 5- to 6-inch-wide disk.

It will be irregular around the circumference and that's good, as all those irregularities will become crunchy goodness. The meat will also shrink by a couple of inches.

7. Gently scrape the patties/wafers off the sheet pan with the spatula and gently drop into the fat. Cook for 1 minute—no more, no less. You can cook up to 3 patties at a time . . . but watch the fat temp and don't let it drop to under 300°F.

8. Remove the fried meat to a paper towel to drain briefly, then move right away to the bun bottom. Place the pickles on top, then the bun top. The goal: bread/mayo/cheese/meat/pickles/cheese/mustard/bread.

9. Consume or wrap in aluminum foil **H** and hold for up to 30 minutes.

Smoky the Meat Loaf

FEEDS 12

½ cup ketchup

¼ cup tomato paste

1 tablespoon dark brown sugar

1 teaspoon garlic powder

2 canned chipotle chiles **P** in adobo
   sauce, chopped fine, plus 1
   tablespoon sauce they're packed in

1 teaspoon dark cocoa powder

6 ounces ruffled kettle-style barbecue
   potato chips

1 medium onion, quartered

1 medium carrot, quartered

1 whole Fresno chile, stemmed and
   seeded

1 tablespoon olive oil

1 teaspoon kosher salt

1 teaspoon dried sage

1 teaspoon dried oregano

1 pound ground chuck*

1 pound ground sirloin

1 pound ground pork

3 large eggs, beaten

SPECIAL EQUIPMENT

Smoker

* Just in case you're asking your butcher to grind this on the spot, ask for a medium or fine grind.

** Okay, if you just can't get to a smoker, go ahead and do this in a 250°F oven. You might also want to add a teaspoon of liquid smoke **P** to the remaining ketchup mixture to glaze with later. Or you could buy a smoker. Just sayin'.

I've been tinkering with this ever since I put an early version on the Interwebs a few years ago. I'm happy to report that I'm finally finished. By the way, if you don't have a smoker, you can roast this loaf on a broiler pan in the oven. But it won't be the same.

1. Combine the ketchup, tomato paste, brown sugar, garlic powder, chipotles, adobo sauce and cocoa powder in a small bowl.

2. Pulse the potato chips in a food processor until they are a coarse bread crumb consistency. Move them to a medium mixing bowl.

3. Next, place the onion, carrot and Fresno chile into the work bowl of the food processor and process until finely chopped.

4. Place a small sauté pan over medium heat and add the olive oil. Once the oil shimmers, add the onion mixture, salt, sage and oregano, and cook, stirring frequently, until the vegetables soften and begin to brown, about 5 minutes. Stir them into the potato chips and cool for 2 to 3 minutes.

5. Add the chuck, sirloin, pork, eggs, and two thirds of the ketchup mixture to the vegetables and use your hands to combine, then move the mixture to a large piece of heavy-duty aluminum foil **H** and shape it into a loaf about 12 x 3½ x 2 inches.

6. Tightly wrap the loaf in heavy-duty aluminum foil. Set aside and leave at room temperature for 1 hour. After 30 minutes, heat your smoker to 250°F.

7. When the hour is up, flip over the meat loaf and poke about 10 holes in the underside of the foil (a metal skewer or paring knife will do) to allow fat to drain out. Flip the loaf back upright and transfer to the smoker, placing a drip pan on the rack immediately below. Load the smoker with one or two chunks of hardwood and cook for 45 minutes.**

8. Open the pack and fold the foil back to create a shallow pan around the meat loaf. Brush with the remaining ketchup mixture and continue smoking until the internal temperature reaches 130°F, about 40 minutes. If the smoke has dissipated, feel free to add another chunk of wood.

9. Remove the meat loaf from the smoker and let rest for 20 minutes before slicing and serving.

Roast Broccoli Hero

FEEDS 4

1 cup sliced bread and butter pickles

½ cup pickle brine (from the bread and butter pickles)

1 garlic clove, minced

1 tablespoon minced fresh ginger

2 tablespoons chili sauce

1 teaspoon sesame oil

1 large head broccoli (about 1 pound), chopped into florets, stalk thinly sliced into rounds

2 tablespoons olive oil

1 teaspoon kosher salt

4 6- to 8-inch French bread rolls

¼ cup mayonnaise *

1 cup prepared fried onions

4 ounces ricotta salata, grated

* If you want to spice things up a bit, mix a teaspoon or two of the pickle marinade into the mayo. Add a little more and you've got a pretty terrific salad dressing.

When I first saw the description of the roasted broccoli sub at No. 7 Sub in NYC, I thought it was crazy talk . . . the rantings of a hipster sandwicheteer. But seeing as it was the specialty of the house, I tried it. Now I have one every time I'm in the city. That version includes a funky Korean salad called muchim with pickled lychee, which isn't that easy to find at the average megamart. So, I replace it here with bread-and-butter pickles. The feta that No. 7 uses I "sub" with ricotta salata, and instead of frying shallots, I crack open a can of an American classic: French's Crispy Fried Onions . . . you know, what your aunt puts on her green bean casserole. Sorry, but I love that stuff and it turns the crunch up to eleven.

1. Heat the oven to 400°F.

2. Combine the pickles, pickle brine, garlic, ginger, chili sauce and sesame oil in a small bowl. Allow the pickles to marinate while you deal with the broccoli.

3. Toss the broccoli with the olive oil and salt in a large bowl, spread into an even layer on a half sheet pan and roast for 15 minutes. Toss and roast for another 15 minutes. When you remove the broccoli from the oven, move a rack under your broiler and heat the broiler to high.

4. Split and lightly toast the rolls under the broiler for 1 to 2 minutes.

5. For each sandwich: Lightly spread mayonnaise on each side of the rolls then evenly distribute the pickles. Next, layer on the broccoli, then the fried onions and top with the ricotta salata.

Roasted Thanksgiving Salad

FEEDS 4 AS A MAIN, FEEDS 6 AS A SIDE

1½ pounds sweet potatoes, peeled
   and cut into ¼-inch pieces
1 pound parsnips,* peeled and cut into
   ¼-inch pieces
1 small red onion, diced
¼ cup plus 2 tablespoons olive oil
2 teaspoons kosher salt
1 cup quinoa P, rinsed in cool water
   and drained**
¼ teaspoon ground cinnamon
3 tablespoons apple cider vinegar
2 tablespoons maple syrup
1 tablespoon Dijon mustard
2 tablespoons fresh thyme leaves
1 teaspoon finely chopped fresh sage
   (about 4 medium leaves)
1 small apple, preferably Gala or
   Honeycrisp, cut into ¼-inch pieces
3 ounces roasted pepitas P

This may be the most nutritiously sound recipe in this book. In fact, if I had to pick one recipe from this book to live on for say a month, it would be . . . Chocolate Chess Pie (page 193)! Just kidding. It would be this. After all, quinoa delivers a complete protein, and sweet potatoes and parsnips deliver just about everything else. And then there are the pepitas, which are packed full of micronutrients, and as you know, doctors hate apples.

By the way . . . this is what Thanksgiving tastes like.

1. Heat the oven to 425°F.

2. Toss the sweet potatoes, parsnips and red onion with 2 tablespoons of the olive oil and 1 teaspoon of the salt, and spread evenly onto two half sheet pans. Roast for 15 minutes, then toss the vegetables, rotate the pans and roast for another 10 minutes, or until the vegetables are tender and golden brown. While the vegetables are roasting, prepare the quinoa.

3. Bring 2 cups water and ½ teaspoon of the salt to a boil in a 2-quart saucepan. Whisk the rinsed quinoa into the boiling water, add the cinnamon, cover, reduce the heat to low and simmer for 15 minutes. Remove from the heat and cool, covered, for 5 minutes. Fluff with a fork.

4. Combine the remaining ¼ cup olive oil, the vinegar, maple syrup, mustard and the remaining ½ teaspoon salt in a small canning jar. Cover and shake the dressing like a martini to emulsify.

5. Toss the warm vegetables, quinoa, thyme, sage and dressing together in a large bowl. Add the apple and pepitas just before serving warm or at room temperature.

* Larger parsnips can have a tough woody core toward their top end, which is not ideal for roasting. Chop the skinny root end into rounds, then cut around the core and chop the remaining sides into ¼-inch cubes.

** Rinsing the quinoa before cooking removes the grain's natural coating (saponin) that would otherwise leave the stuff tasting bitter or soapy. So, don't skip that part!

Fish Sticks and Custard

FEEDS 4

FISH STICKS

1 pound haddock or pollock fillets

1¾ cups panko bread crumbs

3 large eggs

1 tablespoon mayonnaise

1 tablespoon Dijon mustard

½ teaspoon onion powder

½ teaspoon kosher salt

¼ teaspoon cayenne pepper

½ cup all-purpose flour

¼ cup canola oil

CUSTARD

1 large egg yolk

1 cup whole milk

1 tablespoon cornstarch

1 teaspoon Dijon mustard

1 teaspoon fresh lemon juice

½ teaspoon kosher salt

¼ cup finely chopped sour pickles
   (gherkins)

1 teaspoon chopped fresh dill

Ground white pepper

I don't have to explain the significance of this dish to Whovians who remember well the first meal of the regenerated Eleventh Doctor. My version is different in that it's actually tasty . . . even if you don't have two hearts and live in a blue box.

1. Freeze the fish fillets for 30 minutes, or until firm, or if you bought them frozen, thaw for 30 minutes at room temperature. Finely chop the fish and transfer to a bowl with ¾ cup of the panko, 1 of the eggs, the mayonnaise, mustard, onion powder, salt and cayenne pepper. Use your hands or a large spoon to combine. Shape the fish mixture into 1½-ounce finger-shaped sticks. Arrange on a half sheet pan and refrigerate for 30 minutes.

2. Set up your breading station with the flour in a pie pan, the remaining 2 beaten eggs in a second pie pan and the remaining 1 cup panko in pie pan number three. Roll each fish stick in the flour, then the eggs, followed by the panko. Place on a cooling rack set over a sheet pan.

3. Heat the canola oil in a wide nonstick skillet over medium heat (or an electric skillet to medium-high) until it shimmers. Add the fish sticks and cook for 2 to 3 min-utes per side, until golden brown. Remove to paper towels to cool.

4. To prepare the custard, beat the egg yolk in a medium bowl and set aside.

5. Combine the milk, cornstarch, mustard, lemon juice and salt in a 1-quart saucepan and whisk until no lumps remain. Cook, stirring constantly, over medium-low heat until the mixture just starts to boil.

6. Remove from the heat and oh so slowly whisk about half of the hot mixture into the egg yolk, then whisk the now "tempered" egg yolk mixture back into the saucepan.   Cook over low heat, whisking constantly, until the mixture thickens enough to coat the back of a spoon.

7. Remove from the heat, stir in the pickles, dill and white pepper to taste. Cool slightly before serving with the fish sticks.

Slowly heating the proteins in the egg yolk will help prevent it from overcoagulating and curdling the sauce.

If you take a look at the composition of this sauce, it's very close to a tartar sauce, only it's actually a . . . . that's right, TARDIS sauce.

Black Beans/Brown Rice

FEEDS 4

1½ cups medium-grain brown rice

¼ cup olive oil

1½ teaspoons kosher salt

4 large garlic cloves, smashed

¼ teaspoon red pepper flakes [P]

1 small onion, chopped

1 15-ounce can "no salt added" black
    beans, drained and rinsed

1 teaspoon dried oregano

½ teaspoon freshly ground black
    pepper

1 avocado, pitted, peeled and diced**

I try to eat vegetarian at least three or four days a week, and this is a midweek staple. The key is going with brown rice over white, a move that ups the flavor, texture and nutrition.*

1. Heat the oven to 375°F.

2. Spread the rice into an 8-inch square glass baking dish. Stir in 1 tablespoon of the olive oil and 1 teaspoon of the salt.

3. Bring 2½ cups water to a boil in an electric kettle and pour over the rice.*** Cover tightly with heavy-duty aluminum foil [H] and bake on the middle rack of the oven for 1 hour.****

4. Meanwhile, place a 12-inch sauté pan over medium heat. When the pan is hot, add the remaining 3 tablespoons oil to cover the bottom of the pan and add the garlic and red pepper flakes. Cook, stirring frequently, until the garlic is golden brown, 3 to 5 minutes.

5. Add the onion and the remaining ½ teaspoon salt and cook for 1 to 2 minutes, stirring often, until the onion starts to color. Then add the black beans, oregano and black pepper. Cook, stirring frequently, for 6 to 8 minutes.

6. Remove the cover from the rice, fluff with a fork and allow to "steam out" for 2 minutes. Then, serve the beans over the rice, garnished with avocado.

Note: If you want to jazz this dish up, top with a little of the crema on page 15 (BCLT Tacos). By the way, you could also just grab a big flour tortilla and roll this into a burrito!

---

* Take a rice grain out of its husk and you basically have brown rice, that is, white rice wearing a coat of bran . . . and that coat contains most of the nutrients (vitamins, minerals, micronutrients) that rice has to offer. Everything under the coat is just fuel in the form of starch. To make white rice, you simply buff the coat off. The results are pretty, but the nutrition is gone. And that's just sad.

** When ripe, an avocado's flesh will easily separate and can be scooped out of the skin. And by the way, avocados do ripen off the tree. In fact, that's the only way they'll ripen. So store at room temp until they give when squeezed, then move them to the fridge.

*** Obviously there are other ways to boil water; this just happens to be my favored method.

**** That bran coat we were talking about.

Chicken Parmesan Balls

FEEDS 4

3 ounces panko bread crumbs

4 ounces Parmesan cheese, grated

1½ pounds ground chicken

1 large egg, lightly beaten

2 tablespoons herb oil (see page 139)

1 tablespoon dried basil

2 teaspoons garlic powder

2 teaspoons dried parsley

1 teaspoon dried oregano

1 teaspoon kosher salt

Weeknight Spaghetti sauce (page 139)

4 ounces low-moisture mozzarella cheese, grated

When you're in my line of work, personal cuisine can be born on the job. One day we were sitting around the lab and Sarah, my director of digital ops, says, "I want chicken Parmesan." Then I say, "Well, I want meatballs." Then my director of culinary ops looks up and says, "Chicken Parmesan Balls." Then there was a knock on the door, and it was humanity dropping by to say thanks.

1. Heat the oven to 400°F.

2. Mix together ½ ounce of the panko with 1 ounce of the Parmesan in a small bowl. Set aside.

3. Combine the chicken, egg, 1 tablespoon of the herb oil, the remaining 2½ ounces panko, the remaining 3 ounces Parmesan, the basil, garlic powder, parsley, oregano and salt in a large bowl. Using your hands, gently combine until just incorporated, trying not to overwork the meat.

4. Divide the meatball mixture into 28 golf ball–size rounds (1 ounce each) and roll them in the panko mixture.

5. Heat the remaining 1 tablespoon herb oil over medium heat in a 12-inch oven-safe skillet. Brown the meatballs in the herb oil, about 30 seconds on each side, working in batches if needed to avoid crowding the pan. Remove the browned meatballs from the pan and make the spaghetti sauce beginning with step 1, but without cooking the spaghetti.

6. Add the meatballs back to the pan, cover with the grated mozzarella and bake until the meatballs are cooked through, about 10 minutes, and the cheese is melted. Serve over cooked pasta or on top of crispy bread.

Game over, man . . . game over.

"EnchiLasagna" or "Lasagnalada"

2 dried chipotle chiles **P**, stems and
   seeds removed, diced

3 large garlic cloves, minced

2½ teaspoons chili powder

1½ teaspoons toasted cumin seeds,
   freshly ground

2 cups chicken broth

3 cups tomato sauce

½ teaspoon kosher salt

¼ teaspoon freshly ground
   black pepper

FILLING

1 tablespoon canola oil

1 pound boneless, skinless chicken
   breasts or thighs, cubed

1½ cups diced onions

Pinch of kosher salt

1 large garlic clove, minced

1 teaspoon dried oregano

Nonstick cooking spray

18 6-inch corn tortillas

3 cups shredded queso fresco

Doesn't matter how you spell it, it's what happens when you Frankenstein a plate of enchiladas to a lasagna. SCIENCE!

1. Heat the oven to 350°F.

2. To make the sauce, bring the chiles, garlic, chili powder, cumin, chicken broth, tomato sauce, salt and pepper to a boil in a medium saucepan over high heat. When the mixture bubbles, drop the heat to low and simmer for 15 minutes, or until the chiles are just soft.

3. To make the filling, heat the canola oil in a large skillet over medium-high heat and sauté the chicken for 7 to 9 minutes, until cooked through. Transfer to a plate. Add the onions and salt to the same pan, drop the heat to medium-low, and sweat for 4 to 6 minutes. Add the garlic and oregano and cook for 2 to 3 minutes, until the onions are tender. Add the chicken back to the pan and stir to combine. Then, kill the heat.

4. Lube a 13 x 9-inch glass baking dish with nonstick cooking spray, then spread ½ cup of the sauce across the bottom of the dish. Cut the tortillas in half. Dip 12 tortilla halves into the sauce. Arrange the halves on the bottom of the pan in a single layer, with the straight-cut edges

12 HALVES

aligned with the width of the baking dish. Top with half of the chicken mixture and 1 cup of the queso fresco. Repeat the layering, then finish the top with any remaining sauce and the remaining 1 cup queso fresco.

5. Cover the dish with heavy-duty aluminum foil **H** and bake for 30 minutes. Remove the foil and bake for another 10 minutes, or until the queso fresco on top is bubbly and irresistible.

ICEBERG SLAW
Makes approximately 2 cups

A slaw for cabbage haters.

½ cup mayonnaise

4 teaspoons fresh lemon juice
(about 1 lemon's worth)

1 tablespoon Dijon mustard

1 tablespoon hot sauce

2 teaspoons dill pickle brine

½ teaspoon kosher salt

½ teaspoon dried parsley

¼ teaspoon garlic powder

¼ teaspoon black pepper

¼ teaspoon sumac **P**

¼ teaspoon cayenne pepper

1 small head iceberg lettuce, shredded

FRIED OYSTERS

½ cup buttermilk

2 teaspoons hot sauce

24 U.S. farm-raised oysters, shucked

1 quart peanut oil

¾ cup fine ground white cornmeal **P**

¾ cup panko bread crumbs

1½ teaspoons kosher salt

1 teaspoon freshly grated nutmeg **P**

Freshly ground black pepper

TO ASSEMBLE
EACH SANDWICH

4 6- to 8-inch French bread rolls

6 fried oysters

Iceberg Slaw

Oyster Po'boy
MAKES 4 SANDWICHES

Apparently, at some point in my late twenties I ate too many oysters and my body developed an intolerance, which is not the same as an allergy. But it might as well have been because one day I could eat all I wanted and the next day, just one oyster sent me to the hospital. Then, the last time I was in New Orleans, I was at the Parkway Bakery & Tavern and I saw an oyster po'boy go by and my mouth started watering. I decided it was time to roll the dice again and I'm happy to say everyone's doing just fine.

If there's a secret to this sandwich it's using lettuce instead of cabbage in the slaw, which I always make before frying the oysters.

1. Whisk the mayonnaise, lemon juice and the remaining dressing ingredients together in a mixing bowl. Add the iceberg and toss to coat. Cover and refrigerate for 30 minutes.

2. Combine the buttermilk and hot sauce in a small bowl. Add the oysters and soak for 30 minutes to 1 hour.

3. Heat the peanut oil in a 5-quart Dutch oven over medium-high heat until it reaches 370° to 375°F on a deep-fry thermometer **H**.

4. Combine the cornmeal, panko, salt and nutmeg in a medium mixing bowl **M**.

5. Remove the oysters, 1 at a time, from the marinade and shake off the extra moisture. Dredge in the cornmeal mixture, then move to a cooling rack set over a half sheet pan.

6. Once all of the oysters are coated, transfer, 6 at a time, to the hot oil. Fry for 1½ to 2 minutes, until the oysters are golden brown. (Watch your thermometer because the introduction of cold foods will likely pull the temp down a bit.)

7. Carefully transport the fried oysters to a cooling rack inverted over a half sheet pan lined with paper towels. Sprinkle with freshly ground pepper. Bring the oil back to 370° to 375°F and repeat with the remaining oysters.

8. Split the rolls in half lengthwise. Tear out a bit of the bread from the center of each roll, creating a trough. Set 6 oysters on one side. Top with ½ cup of the slaw and the top of the roll.

9. Consume. Notice how the slaw is kinda gooshy (in a good way) and how that contrasts with the crunch of the oysters. Pulling some of the bread out of the middle will help the sandwich stay together, but you're still going to need a roll of paper towels to eat this thing.

The Final Turkey

FEEDS 8 TO 10

I have arrived at my final turkey.

It may not be your final turkey, but after years of searching, this is where I get off. The procedure is Zen-simple, and yet when followed, it produces perfectly cooked meat—meaning breast meat at 158°F and dark meat at 178°F. It is flavorful, it is juicy, it is, well . . . I refuse to use the word "perfect," but there it is. There is, however, one catch. A large Dutch oven is required, specifically a Lodge 12- or 14-inch-deep camp oven; a Dutch oven with three legs and a lid that's made for stacking charcoal on. Should you own one of these anyway? Heck yeah you should. And don't be freaked by the legs; most of the time I'm using this right on the floor of the oven. But even if you don't make up big pots of chili or campfire biscuits or beans for fifty on a regular basis, you'll want to own this hulking fallout shelter for hamsters for no reason other than turkey. Speaking of, notice the weight of said bird. I don't mess with the big birds anymore because they take too long to cook, they tend to dry out by the time they hit safe temperatures, and besides, who the heck has an oven that big anyway. I keep to medium birds in the 12- to 14-pound range, which are plenty big for 8 to 10 people. If you have more guests, heck, cook two.

1. Place 1 cup kosher salt in a cooler and dissolve in 2 liters hot water. When you're certain the very last crystal has vanished, add 4 liters cold water.

2. Unwrap a *frozen* turkey and place it, breast-side down, in your vessel. Close the vessel and leave it at room temperature for 36 hours. * After about 8 you should be able to remove the neck and giblet bag. If you like giblet gravy, save them; if not . . . you know what to do.

3. After 36 hours, drain the bird and let sit at room temp for about 1 hour.

4. Place the Dutch oven (lid on) either on the floor of the oven or position the legs so that it can sit on the bottom rack.

5. Heat the oven to 500°F a good 45 minutes prior to cooking so that the Dutch oven is fully loaded, thermally speaking.

6. Cross the ends of the turkey's legs and secure them with a short piece of butcher's twine tied preferably with a surgeon's knot, though I suppose a locking clove hitch would work if you prefer.

7. Lightly oil the bird (canola is fine) and sprinkle with 2 teaspoons kosher salt.

8. When both inner and outer ovens are scorching hot, quickly remove the lid of the Dutch oven, being careful to avoid any smoke that may billow out. **

9. Drop the bird, spine down, into the Dutch oven and replace the lid. If the bird is so big that the lid doesn't quite close all the way, don't worry about it. As long as the gap isn't more than a quarter of an inch it won't matter. Just smack that sucker down.

10. Close the oven door and cook for 20 minutes.

11. Open the oven door, remove the Dutch oven lid, close the oven door and cook for another 20 minutes.

12. Remove the pot to the cooktop or other safe surface and replace the lid. If your bird was a little big for the lid to start, just cover with a couple layers of heavy-duty aluminum foil **H**, then use a kitchen towel to crimp the foil onto the sides of the Dutch oven. Spread the towel on top of this to hold the foil down and add some insulation. Wait another 20 minutes.

13. Insert the stem of an instant-read thermometer **H** into the deepest part of the breast. It should read 158°F. ***

14. Remove the lid or foil and let the turkey rest in the pot for 5 minutes.

15. Insert the big end of a large wooden spoon into the turkey cavity and use that to carefully lift the bird out to a cutting board.

16. Carve and consume.

Oh jeeze, I can hear the helicopters now coming in low out of the sunset full of worrywarts and lawyers and (shudder) bloggers to harp in perfect harmony about how I'm ignoring the very fundamentals of food sanitation. Well, riddle me this: A frozen bird that size goes into a cold salt brine in the cooler; how long will it take for the solution to rise above 40°F and into the dread "danger zone"? That's right . . . about 24 hours. Besides, how many bacteria can thrive in a salt solution? On this planet, not many. So if you want to refrigerate your turkey as it brines, fine by me, but this is how I do it, and it's my book and that's that.

** In this instance, the rack is a good option because it will help facilitate loading and unloading the bird.

*** Okay, "billow" is probably a bit dramatic. But odds are there will be a little because a well-cared-for Dutch oven always has some oil on its surface, and at this temperature, some of that will become vapor, That is, smoke.

**** Yes, I know that 165°F is the instant-kill temp for salmonella, but those suckers die at lower temperatures as well, as long as the exposure is long enough. If you're deeply concerned, add 5 minutes to the first cooking phase . . . but I wouldn't.

Not Just Another Kale Salad

FEEDS 4

1 bunch lacinato kale, stems removed, cut into ribbons

1 bunch fresh flat-leaf parsley, stems removed, roughly chopped

1 small shallot, frenched **M**

4 tablespoons extra-virgin olive oil

2 tablespoons fresh lemon juice

2 large garlic cloves, minced

2 ounces anchovies **P** in olive oil, approximately ½ 4.25-ounce can, finely chopped*

3 ounces firm feta cheese

2 tablespoons finely chopped Quick Preserved Lemons (page 167)

1 cup Crispy Chickpeas (page 102), crushed

Freshly ground black pepper

Kale is a unique dark leafy green that can stand up to heavy dressings and yet is tender enough to be eaten raw, hence its popularity in salads. This member of the cabbage family comes in three common market forms: curly, red (also curly), and lacinato, aka Tuscan, aka *cavolo nero*, aka "dinosaur" kale. This latter specimen has long, relatively flat leaves and is my preferred kale for this application.

1. Toss the kale, parsley and shallot with 2 tablespoons of the olive oil and let sit for 10 minutes.

2. Meanwhile, puree the remaining 2 tablespoons olive oil, the lemon juice, garlic, anchovies and 1 ounce of the feta in a food processor. Pour the dressing over the kale, then toss in the preserved lemon, chickpeas and the remaining 2 ounces feta.

3. Marinate at room temp for 1 hour before serving with freshly ground pepper.**

* Stop it! I know what you're thinking, and yes, you need them and no, the salad won't taste fishy and you must trust me on this.

** If you want to make it ahead, just hold out the chickpeas and refrigerate the salad for up to 4 hours. I'd still give it time to come to room temp before serving, though.

AFTER-NOON

Green Grape Cobbler

FEEDS 8 TO 10

A bunch of years ago, I demo'd at the Orange County Fair out in California, and the theme that year was grapes. Research ensued and someone in the kitchen stumbled over a grape pie that, with some tinkering, became this dish, which combines grapy with salty and creamy and crunchy and sticky and boozy. Kids love it! (Don't worry, it's only a couple tablespoons of brandy.)

1 pound seedless green grapes, halved

½ cup honey

2 tablespoons brandy **B**

2 tablespoons fresh lime juice

5 ounces vanilla wafers

4 ounces toasted walnuts (extra for garnishing, optional)

¼ teaspoon kosher salt

6 tablespoons (¾ stick) unsalted butter, melted, plus 12 tablespoons (1½ sticks)

16 ounces sour cream

1¼ cups packed dark brown sugar

2 tablespoons vanilla extract

½ teaspoon coarse sea salt, such as Maldon **P**

1. Combine the grapes, honey, brandy and lime juice in a zip-top bag, seal and refrigerate for 8 to 12 hours.

2. Finely grind the vanilla wafers, walnuts and salt in a food processor for 15 seconds. Drizzle in the melted butter and pulse 6 to 8 times to combine. Press the vanilla wafer mixture into an even, compact layer in an 11 x 7-inch glass baking dish. Set aside.

3. Whisk together the sour cream, ½ cup of the brown sugar and the vanilla in a large mixing bowl. Drain the grapes and discard the liquid. Gently stir the grapes into the sour cream mixture, then spread the mixture over the crust and set aside.

4. Combine the remaining ¾ cup brown sugar with the remaining 12 tablespoons butter in a small saucepan and bring to a boil over medium-high heat. Cook for 1 minute longer, then pour the sugar mixture (caramel) over the grape mixture. Do not stir! Cool at room temperature for 15 minutes, then sprinkle the sea salt on top. Chill for 1 hour before serving.

BUTTERSCOTCH PUDDIN'

[FEEDS 6]

ALTHOUGH SOME HISTORIANS ARGUE THAT THIS DISH DOES INDEED HAIL FROM SCOTLAND, I THINK IT'S FAR MORE LIKELY THE "SCOTCH" IS A BASTARDIZATION OF "SCORCH"; WHICH MAKES SENSE AS EARLY RECIPES CALL FOR ESSENTIALLY BURNING BUTTER AND BROWN SUGAR TOGETHER. ONE THING'S FOR SURE, BUTTERSCOTCH HASN'T ACTUALLY CONTAINED SCOTCH WHISKEY... UNTIL NOW.
YOU'RE WELCOME.

2 tablespoons (1/4 stick) unsalted butter
6 ounces dark brown sugar
2 cups whole milk
1 cup heavy cream
1/2 teaspoon kosher salt
2 ounces granulated sugar
4 large egg yolks
1 ounce corn starch (1/4 cup)
1 ounce Scotch whiskey [B]
1 tablespoon vanilla extract
1 teaspoon smoked salt [P]

1. Melt the butter in a 2-quart saucier or saucepan over medium-high heat. Add the brown sugar and cook, stirring occasionally, until the sugar has dissolved and the butter smells nutty, 1-2 minutes.

2. Pour in the milk, cream and kosher salt and bring to a simmer. Remove from the heat and cool slightly.

3. Meanwhile, whisk the granulated sugar and egg yolks together in a large bowl until the mixture is smooth and thick. Add the cornstarch and whisk smooth.

4. Temper the warm dairy mixture into the egg mixture by slowly ladling about ½ cup of the warm dairy mixture into the egg mixture, whisking constantly. Repeat ladling in the dairy, whisking until about a third has been worked into the eggs. At this point you can add the remaining dairy all at once.

5. Strain the pudding base back into the saucepan and return to medium heat. Continue cooking, stirring occasionally, until the mixture begins to bubble and thicken. Remove from the heat and stir in the scotch and vanilla.

6. Pour the thickened pudding into six small ramekins, place a piece of plastic wrap on the surface of each pudding, and refrigerate until thoroughly set, at least 4 hours.

7. Sprinkle on a bit of the flaky salt just before serving.

SLOWLY HEATING THE YOLKS WILL HELP TO PREVENT PROTEIN OVERCOAGULATION AND THE GRAININESS THAT CAN RESULT.

(LIKE CHILDHOOD ONLY WITHOUT THE SCREAMING)

Brown on Blonde

MAKES TWELVE 2-INCH-SQUARE BARS

170 grams unsalted butter

100 grams walnuts

55 grams pecans

272 grams all-purpose flour

6 grams baking powder

3 grams kosher salt

55 grams almond butter

346 grams dark brown sugar

2 large eggs

1 large egg yolk

1 tablespoon vanilla extract

There was a time I felt that blondies were nothing more than brownies somebody forgot to put chocolate in. Then one day I went to make brownies and actually didn't have any chocolate, so I made blondies . . . really bad blondies. Intrigued, I went to work trying to get the proper balance of buttery/nutty/chewy/crispy. The secret is to use a combination of nuts and to fry them in the butter before assembly.

1. Crank the oven to 350°F. Coat the insides of an 8-inch square baking pan with non-stick cooking spray and line with a sling of parchment paper.

2. Melt the butter in an 8-inch sauté pan over medium heat. When it's done bubbling, add the walnuts and pecans and cook until the nuts are toasted and the butter smells nutty, 5 to 7 minutes.

3. Meanwhile, whisk together the flour, baking powder and salt in a small bowl.

4. Place a fine-mesh strainer over a large heatproof bowl and strain the butter away from the nuts. Set both aside to cool for 30 minutes. Then, chop the nuts coarsely and set aside.

5. While you're waiting, beat the almond butter into the cooled butter, followed by the brown sugar, eggs, egg yolk and vanilla. Beat until completely smooth, about 1 minute, then stir in the flour mixture. Finish by folding in the nuts and transferring to the prepared pan. The batter will be thick, so I suggest a rubber or silicone spatula.

6. Bake for 30 to 35 minutes, until the edges are deeply brown and the top is dry and cracked. Remove the pan and cool on a rack for about 30 minutes. Remove from the pan, slice into squares and devour with plenty of frosty almond milk.

Kick-in-the-Pants Smoothie

MAKES 2 SMOOTHIES . . . OR 1 REALLY BIG ONE

180 grams unsweetened almond milk

1 medium banana (frozen)*

10 pitted dates P

25 grams dark agave

5 grams unsweetened Dutch-process cocoa powder (1½ teaspoons)

Pinch of kosher salt

250 grams ice (about 8 ounces)

150 grams Cold Brew Coffee (page 39)

* Any time I have bananas starting to overripen, I peel them, wrap them in plastic wrap, and freeze them. That way, I always have smoothie fodder, and I never have rotten bananas.

Dates, that is, the fruit (drupes, actually) of the date palm, were long at the outer frontier of my culinary universe. Sure, I'd stuff them every now and then as hors d'oeuvres, but they didn't really play a role in my daily food life. Then I stumbled across a study about their nutrition and I decided to get with it. Loads of fiber, vitamins, minerals, amino acids and a lot of (nearly 80 percent) sugar. And yet . . . apparently dates don't drive up blood sugar and are therefore low-glycemic-index foods, which means no sugar crash. And then there's the flavor. When dates are combined with coffee and relatively small amounts of cocoa, you get . . . chocolate. Seriously, if someone was allergic to chocolate but wanted to taste it, I'd make them this. If you want it a little less sweet, drop the agave down to 15 grams. And yes, I really do weigh all this. I just put the blender carafe on the scale H, zero it out, and load it up.

1. Combine the almond milk, banana, dates, agave, cocoa powder and salt in a blender. Cover and slowly run the device up to medium speed for about 1 minute. Believe it or not, this will break up the dates better than a higher speed. After a minute, boost to high for another 30 seconds or so. Stop, add the ice and cold brew, and blend smooth.

2. Serve immediately and marvel at the chocolaty goodness, despite the fact there's only about a teaspoon of cocoa powder.

Chewy Peanut Butter Cookie

MAKES 16 COOKIES

A one-bowl, no-mixer cookie that's also gluten free (bows deeply). *

1 cup smooth peanut butter
½ cup packed light brown sugar
½ cup granulated sugar
1 large egg
1 teaspoon baking soda
1 teaspoon vanilla extract
¼ teaspoon kosher salt

1. Heat the oven to 350°F. Line two half sheet pans with parchment paper and set aside.
2. Beat together the peanut butter, brown sugar and granulated sugar until well combined with a wooden spoon in a large bowl. Add the egg, baking soda, vanilla and salt and beat until well combined.
3. Roll the dough into 1-ounce balls, place 8 per prepared sheet pan, then flatten with the tines of a fork. Bake for 10 minutes, or until the cookies look dry and are just lightly browned. Cool the cookies for 2 minutes on the sheet pans.

* I honestly don't care about the gluten-free part. I'm just looking for excuses to eat cookies.

Thai Iced Tea

MAKES 1 QUART, FEEDS 4

Next to coffee, Thai tea is my favorite beverage on earth. Problem is, dye-packed, quick-brew mixes have become so prevalent that finding a suitable sample out in the world has become tough. The answer, of course, is make your own. I like mine to have a tang to it, so I start with Earl Grey tea rather than standard black tea, and I include tamarind pulp. Is it nice and clear like Southern sweet tea? Nope. But since I always put a little half-and-half in mine, I care not.

5 cups filtered or bottled water

6 Earl Grey tea bags

1 ounce fresh tamarind pulp, smashed*

8 green cardamom pods

8 whole cloves

2 whole star anise pods P

1 cinnamon stick

½ vanilla bean or 1 teaspoon vanilla extract

¼ teaspoon kosher salt

½ cup sugar

½ cup half-and-half

1. Bring the water to a boil in a 2-quart saucepan. Remove from the boil and add the tea bags, tamarind, cardamom, cloves, star anise, cinnamon, vanilla and salt.

2. Cover the saucepan with a lid and steep the tea for 20 minutes.

3. Remove the tea bags and strain out the spices and vanilla bean (if using).

4. Add the sugar and stir to dissolve.

5. Chill the Thai tea base for at least 8 hours before serving over ice with a splash of half-and-half.**

* To get the pulp out of a tamarind pod, just crack the thin outer case and remove the pulpy interior. Some folks pick out the seeds, but I don't bother. Two pods usually yield the correct amount. If you want to use packaged paste, that's fine too.

** Canned milk is more authentic since it was probably the only dairy that colonists could get their hands on when they moved into Southeast Asia. But, I think the fat content of half-and-half is better at balancing the tannins in the tea.

Hotel L'Americain
482- 527 Yaowaraj Rd
SAMPHANTAWONG BANGKOK
10100 THAILAND

ALTON BROWN
P.O. BOX 2001
ATLANTA, GA 30709
U.S.A. (CHECK, YEAH)

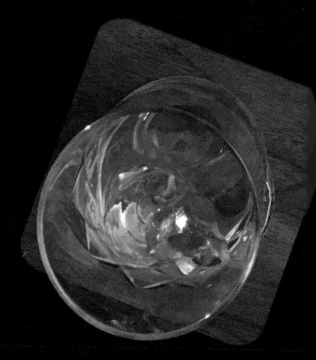

Savory Greek Yogurt Dip

MAKES 1 QUART

I'm a big-time dipper. I'd probably eat a pinecone if I had the right dip. Come to think of it, this might be just that dip. Also good for schmearing on burgers, wings and falafel, and, of course, it will upgrade nearly everything in the vegetable department. You can also mix it with chopped garlic and cucumbers into a fast tzatziki-like sauce.

1 quart plain Greek yogurt

1 tablespoon finely chopped fresh flat-leaf parsley

1 tablespoon finely chopped fresh mint

1 teaspoon ground cumin or smoked paprika **P**

1 teaspoon grated lemon zest

1 teaspoon kosher salt

½ teaspoon freshly ground black pepper

Combine the yogurt, parsley, mint, cumin, lemon zest, salt and pepper in a medium bowl. Transfer to an airtight container, cover and refrigerate for up to 10 days.

Crispy Chickpeas

MAKES 2 CUPS

2 15-ounce cans chickpeas
2 tablespoons olive oil
1 teaspoon kosher salt
1 teaspoon sumac **P**
¼ teaspoon cayenne pepper

1. Rinse the chickpeas under cold water in the basket of your salad spinner. Drain, then spin in the spinner to dry even more. Move to a paper towel–lined half sheet pan. Top with another layer of paper towels, roll up and pat to dry even more. In case you don't see the pattern here, what we're after is dry!

2. Remove the paper towels from the sheet pan and toss the chickpeas with the olive oil and salt. Put the pan (with the chickpeas) in a cold oven, set a timer for 30 minutes and crank the oven to 350°F.

3. Turn the oven off and leave the chickpeas inside to dry and become crispy, about 1 hour.

4. Toss the still-warm chickpeas with the sumac and cayenne pepper. Cool completely before storing.

5. Devour as a snack or use unseasoned in Not Just Another Kale Salad (page 84).

Red, Red Wine (Sangria)

MAKES 12 SERVINGS

Sangria is not only my favorite summer punch, it's probably the simplest and cheapest one to fabricate. And if there's ever been a more food-friendly quaff, I can't think of what it would be.

2 cups chopped fruit, such as apples, pears, strawberries or plums, plus more for garnish

3 tablespoons sugar

1 cup brandy **B**

2 bottles red wine, preferably Rioja or Grenache blend

½ cup fresh orange juice

½ cup lemon-lime soda

1. Combine the fruit, sugar and brandy in a 3-quart pitcher and stir until the sugar dissolves. Refrigerate for 6 to 8 hours.

2. When you're ready to serve, add the wine, orange juice and lemon-lime soda to the pitcher and stir to combine. Pour over ice and garnish with more fruit.

Grenache is one of the most plentiful grapes of the wine world, but due to some specific deficiencies (acidity for one), it's rarely bottled on its own, but rather blended. Many wines from the southern Rhône employ high percentages of Grenache, as do others from Spain. Increasingly, you see it in wines called GSMs or Grenache/Syrah/Mourvèdre blends.

Zissou's* Buffet of Underwater Delights

FEEDS 6 TO 8

¼ cup low-sodium soy sauce

2 tablespoons Asian chili garlic sauce, such as Huy Fong**

1 tablespoon fish sauce P, such as Red Boat

1 tablespoon Chinese five-spice powder P

1 pound small red potatoes, halved if 2 inches or larger in diameter

1 bunch scallions, trimmed and halved

1 head garlic, cloves separated but not peeled

1 ounce fresh ginger, peeled and cut into ¼-inch slices

2 ears of corn, shucked and halved

8 ounces Chinese sausage (lap xeong), cut into 1-inch pieces***

1 large lime, quartered

1 1½- to 2-pound lobster

8 ounces (31/40 count) head-on, tail-on shrimp

8 ounces small clams, such as littleneck

8 ounces mussels, debearded and rinsed

SPECIAL EQUIPMENT

A pot in the 8-quart range with a steamer insert or basket H

I typically prepare a massive pot of this out in the yard using the derrick I devised for frying turkeys, but this version has been recalibrated for indoor cookery.

1. Place 2 quarts water, the soy sauce, chili sauce, fish sauce, five-spice, potatoes, scallions, garlic and ginger inside the pot and bring to a boil over high heat.

2. Meanwhile, into the steamer insert, place in this order the corn, sausage, lime, lobster, shrimp, clams and finally the mussels.

3. When the goodness in the pot is boiling, lower the steamer insert into the pot. Cover and cook for 8 to 10 minutes, until the clams and mussels just open.****

4. Lift the steamer basket out of the pot enough to allow any liquid to drain. Then dump the contents onto a large platter, into a bowl, or even right onto a table lined with newspaper. Use a spider H to fish out the potatoes onto the serving vessel. Ladle the broth into cups or bowls and serve the lot.

* I am a lifelong member of the Zissou Society.

** Although the most popular form of this sauce comes in a jar with a rooster on it, don't confuse it with sambal oelek (see Chili-Glazed Wings [page 203], Cockpit Shrimp Cocktail [page 195]), which also has a chicken on it. The difference: Chili garlic sauce contains garlic, sambal does not.

*** Chinese-style sausages come in myriad styles but can generally be divided into fresh and dried or aged. The first is more like Italian sausage and the second like . . . well, a Slim Jim. You want to go with the one that looks the least shriveled.

**** If the pot/liquid combo is right, the bivalves will be above the level of the liquid and will steam rather than boil.

Cucumber Lime Yogurt Pops

MAKES 8 TO 12 POPS

I live in the South. If you haven't spent any time down here, allow me to inform you that it gets freakin' hot. Have you ever seen *The Walking Dead*? See how those people sweat? That's not because they're plagued by zombies, that's because they're plagued by Georgia heat. If only they realized relief comes at the end of a creeping vine of the Cucurbitaceae family upon which grows a fruit called the cucumber. The fact that these things are frozen doesn't hurt.

1 pound cucumbers, seeded and
    chopped
½ cup plain Greek yogurt
½ cup Demerara sugar  P
1 large lime, zested and juiced
½ teaspoon chile powder
¼ teaspoon kosher salt

SPECIAL EQUIPMENT
Popsicle molds,
Popsicle sticks

1. Combine the cucumbers, yogurt,
sugar, lime zest, lime juice, chile powder and salt in a food processor. Puree
for 30 seconds, stop, scrape down the
sides of the food processor bowl and
puree until smooth.

2. Pour the mixture into Popsicle
molds, add the Popsicle sticks, and
freeze for 4 hours, or until solid. Store
in a zip-top bag in the freezer for up
to 2 weeks.

It's been proven that spicy foods
can cool you down by increasing
blood flow and making you sweat.
And in this case, the chili powder
tastes good too.

Fiery Ginger Ale Concentrate

MAKES ABOUT 18 OUNCES SYRUP, ENOUGH FOR ABOUT 8 SERVINGS

I like ginger ale, but most commercial examples are just too darned sweet for me. By mixing this syrup with soda water, I can dial it in exactly the way I like. And yes . . . ginger and cinnamon.

125 grams (4.4 ounces) crystallized ginger **P**, coarsely chopped
1 cinnamon stick, lightly crushed
575 grams water (just make it 20 ounces if you like)

1. Bring all the ingredients to a boil over high heat and keep it there for 2 minutes. Then kill the heat and allow to steep for 1 hour.

2. Strain out the solids, cool completely and refrigerate in a sealed container for up to 1 month.

3. When you desire a glass of refreshing goodness, simply mix 2 ounces syrup with 6 to 8 ounces of cold sparkling water. If you're feeling especially naughty and don't have anywhere to go, mix 2 ounces syrup with 2 ounces vodka and top it off with the soda.

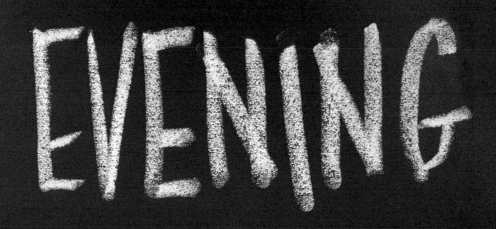

EVENING

Onion Oxtail Soup

FEEDS 4

3 pounds yellow onions (2 to 3 large)

2 tablespoons kosher salt

1 tablespoon dark brown sugar

½ teaspoon baking soda

2 pounds beef oxtails (4 large)

1 cup red wine

5 thyme sprigs, tied into a bundle

1½ quarts beef broth

¼ teaspoon black pepper (a few grinds)

Groovy Gruyère Sticks (recipe follows)

1. Heat the oven to 300°F.

2. Halve and peel the onions, then slice on a mandoline **H** set to 3 millimeters and place in a bowl. Toss with 1 tablespoon of the salt, the brown sugar and baking soda, then place in a large colander for 15 minutes, tossing occasionally.

3. Meanwhile, place a heavy 4-quart Dutch oven over high heat for 5 minutes.

4. Season the oxtails with 2 teaspoons of the remaining salt and sear in the Dutch oven. Set the seared oxtails aside, but don't wipe the pot out . . . you'll need a little fat for the onions.

5. Wring as much moisture out of the onions as possible by pressing them down into the bottom of the colander.

6. Sauté the onions in the Dutch oven over high heat until they brown, about 8 min-

utes. When the onions are brown, add the wine and cook for 5 minutes.

7. Place the oxtail meat and thyme bundle on top of the onions. Pour in the broth (should just cover the oxtails). Lid the pot, place in the center of the oven, and simmer for 3 to 4 hours, until the oxtails pull apart easily.

8. Remove the oxtails and thyme from the soup. When cool enough to handle, remove the meat from the oxtails and chop coarsely.

9. Add the oxtail meat back to the soup and bring back to a simmer before serving. Taste and correct the seasoning with the remaining 1 teaspoon salt and the black pepper.

Groovy Gruyère Sticks

8 ounces grated Gruyère cheese

4 thin sourdough bread slices, about ¼ inch thick

I know that at this point, a few of you are wondering what the heck happened to the big, melty, cheesy crouton that's supposed to cap the crock? Oh, you mean the soggy, stringy, goo heap that is typically used to camouflage a substandard soup? The way I see it, a little cheese toast on the side is a better way to go because you get all the flavor and some crunch, and frankly, who doesn't like cheese toast? Here's how I do it.

1. Heat your panini press **H** to high.

2. Take 2 ounces of the Gruyère and sprinkle it into two bread-shaped beds on either side of the panini press. Immediately lay 1 piece of bread onto each bed, top each with an additional ounce of the

cheese, and press for 1 minute. Immediately remove the cheese toasts to a cooling rack and repeat with the remaining cheese and bread.

3. Once the cheese toasts cool, cut into sticks and serve with Onion Oxtail Soup.

Chicken Piccata

FEEDS 6

3 ounces white wine (I usually go with a Sauvignon Blanc)

4 ounces chicken broth

1 lemon, sliced into 8 wafer-thin slices, plus ½ lemon for 1½ tablespoons juice

8 boneless, skinless chicken thighs

2 teaspoons kosher salt

½ teaspoon freshly ground black pepper, plus more for serving

1 cup all-purpose flour

3 tablespoons unsalted butter

2 tablespoons olive oil

8 ounces white button mushrooms, sliced thin

3 tablespoons capers, drained but not rinsed

2 tablespoons chopped fresh flat-leaf parsley

I used to think that *piccata* meant "sharp" and referred to the tang of the sauce. Truth is, it refers more to the shaping and pounding of the meat, which is typically chicken breast. I never send a breast to do what thighs could do better (and cheaper), and this dish certainly falls into that category. If you don't want to mess with boning, go with boneless, skinless thighs; otherwise, you'll need a thin sharp knife for boning.

1. Combine the white wine, broth and lemon juice in a beaker or measuring cup. Set aside.

2. Season the thighs with 1 teaspoon of the salt and the pepper.

3. Place the flour in a gallon freezer bag and add one thigh to the bag. Seal, and shake to coat. Then open the bag just enough to allow air out. Place the thigh on a sturdy counter or cutting board and flatten that sucker with a meat pounder, flipping the bag once during the process, until the thigh is about ¼ inch thick. Remove to a plate and repeat with the rest of the thighs.

4. Place a heavy, 12-inch straight-sided sauté pan with a tight-fitting lid over high heat for 1 minute.

5. Add 1 tablespoon each of the butter and the oil to the pan. When the butter just stops bubbling, carefully add 4 of the thighs. Cook, gently shaking the pan, for 90 seconds, then flip and repeat for another 90 seconds.

6. Remove the chicken from the pan, add another 1 tablespoon each of the butter and oil, and when the butter is melted, add the remaining 4 thighs and cook as before.

7. Remove the chicken from the pan and immediately add the mushrooms and the remaining 1 teaspoon salt. Toss or stir to sauté for 2 minutes, or until the mushrooms start to turn golden on the cooked sides.

8. Stir the mushrooms out to the circumference of the pan and add the capers right into the middle. Stir, cooking for another 1 minute.

9. Add the chicken back to the pan and reduce the heat to low. Distribute the lemon slices across the top of the chicken, add the wine mixture and slap on the lid. Braise thusly for 5 to 7 minutes, until the chicken is cut-with-a-fork tender.

10. Evacuate the thighs (discard the lemon slices atop) to a serving platter. Increase the heat to high and add the remaining 1 tablespoon butter to the sauce. Boil gently, stirring constantly until it reaches sauce consistency . . . about 30 seconds, then pour it over the chicken. Grind on some more pepper and top with the parsley. Serve with rice or noodles, if you like.

Cocoa Nib Vinaigrette

MAKES 3/4 CUP

2 tablespoons cocoa nibs*
4 tablespoons extra-virgin olive oil
3 tablespoons balsamic vinegar
2 tablespoons minced shallot
½ teaspoon kosher salt
½ teaspoon red pepper flakes **P**

SALAD SUGGESTIONS TO DRESS IN COCOA NIB VINAIGRETTE

8 ounces torn butter lettuce
1 avocado, pitted, peeled and diced
2 oranges, suprêmed
2 ounces dried cherries
1 ounce bittersweet chocolate shavings
2 tablespoons cocoa nibs

OR

8 ounces chopped endive or radicchio
1 cup halved green grapes
2 ounces crumbled cooked bacon
2 ounces crumbled blue cheese
1 ounce bittersweet chocolate shavings
2 tablespoons cocoa nibs

OR

8 ounces spring mix
1 cup halved strawberries
2 ounces crumbled goat cheese
1 ounce bittersweet chocolate shavings
2 tablespoons cocoa nibs

Children of the world, rejoice! I, Alton Brown, have invented a salad with chocolate! Chocolate, I say! Worship me and together we . . . Sorry. So, cocoa nibs, those roasted seed things that chocolate comes from, are really good in salad.

1. Pulse the cocoa nibs in a spice grinder 4 or 5 times, until finely ground.

2. Combine the ground cocoa nibs and the olive oil in a 1-quart saucepan, and heat on low for 2 to 3 minutes, until warm and fragrant.

3. Add the vinegar, shallot, salt and red pepper flakes, and let sit for about 1 hour, until cooled to room temperature.

4. Transfer to a jar, twist on the lid, and shake like crazy to combine.

* Available at most quality megamarts these days, as well as the Interwebs . . . just like everything else.

Kimchi Crab Cakes

MAKES TWELVE 2-OUNCE CAKES, FEEDS 6

½ cup mayonnaise

1 lime, zested and then cut into
   6 wedges

1 large egg

3 ounces kimchi, drained and finely
   chopped

½ teaspoon freshly ground black
   pepper

½ teaspoon kosher salt

3 ounces panko bread crumbs

8 ounces lump crabmeat (aka "backfin
   meat")

8 ounces jumbo lump crabmeat (aka
   "the good stuff")

¼ cup canola oil

Don't worry . . . you're not going to have to make spicy, fermented cabbage. Mind you, it's delicious and relatively simple to make, but the truth is, the kimchi I buy at my local Korean market is way better than any I've ever made. Even if you're not lucky enough to have a Korean market nearby, most decent megamarts carry it these days. And here's the shocker: Kimchi goes well with crab.

1. Set a cooling rack inside a half-sheet pan and set aside.

2. Whisk the mayonnaise, lime zest, egg, kimchi, pepper and salt together in a large bowl, then fold in 1½ ounces of the panko and the lump and jumbo lump crabmeat.

3. Fill a pie pan with the remaining 1½ ounces panko. Divide the crab mixture into twelve 2-ounce portions and shape into patties. Coat the crab cakes in the panko, then place on the prepared cooling rack. Refrigerate for 30 minutes.

4. Heat the canola oil in a 12-inch sauté pan over medium heat. When the oil shimmers, cook the crab cakes, 4 at a time, for 3 minutes per side, or until golden brown. Remove to a clean cooling rack set over paper towels to drain. Repeat with the remaining crab cakes.

5. Serve immediately with the lime wedges. Sauce?!?! We don't need no stinkin' sauce!

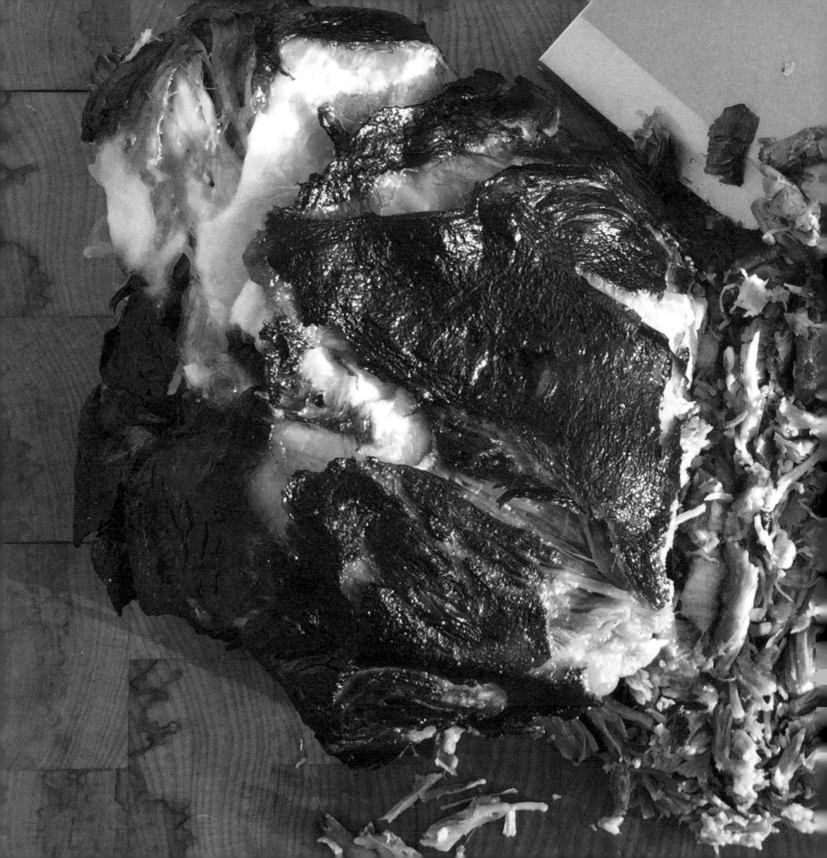

Barbecue Pork Butt

MAKES 4 TO 6 POUNDS PULLED PORK

12 ounces kosher salt

8 ounces molasses

8- to 10-pound boneless pork butt

SPECIAL EQUIPMENT

Smoker and 4 ounces hickory or oak wood chunks.

And you really need a decent instant-read/meat thermometer **H** . . . not that that's "special" equipment.

Barbecue purists call this cheating. I call it freakin' awesome. The smoke is for flavor; the foil time is for texture. If you have an electric smoker that runs to 300°F, feel free to use it for the entire cooking time. But do not skip the foil.

1. Stir 3 quarts water, the salt, and molasses together in a large 12-quart container until the salt dissolves. Move 2 cups of the brine into a zip-top bag. Add the pork butt to the remaining brine and weigh it down with the bag. Refrigerate for 8 to 10 hours.

2. Remove the pork from the brine and pat dry. Discard the brine.

3. Heat the smoker to 225°F.

4. Load the pig part into the smoker and add the wood chunks according to the manufacturer's instructions.

5. Once the meat reaches 140°F (after 3 to 4 hours), crank the oven to 300°F.

6. Wrap the pork in heavy-duty aluminum foil **H** and transfer to a sheet pan or roasting pan. Place on the center rack and cook until the pork reaches an internal temperature of 200°F and is tender and pulling apart easily, 3 to 5 hours.

7. Remove from the oven, loosen the foil so heat can escape, and park at room temp for 30 minutes before shredding with a couple of big forks and serving to a grateful world.

Actually part of the shoulder. It's named "butt" after the type of barrel that commonly housed it.

I go with white bread and bread and butter pickles. As for sauce . . . we don't need no stinkin' sauce.

Mussels-O-Miso

2 pounds mussels

1 tablespoon vegetable oil

6 shishito peppers, sliced

2 tablespoons fresh ginger, minced

2 large garlic cloves, minced

½ cup chicken broth

¼ cup brown miso paste

1 tablespoon fish sauce **P**

1 tablespoon dark brown sugar

2 bottles lager beer (½ cup for the
  recipe, the rest to drink with it)

1 tablespoon harissa paste

3 limes, 2 juiced and 1 quartered,
  for serving

½ cup fresh cilantro leaves, chopped

This may seem like a rather exotic dish, given the ingredient list, but several of the odder ingredients here are multitaskers worthy of permanent residency in your kitchen.

1. Rinse and scrub the mussels under cool running water. Remove any "beards" by pulling the fiber down toward the hinge end. Discard the beards and any open mussels that do not close within 30 seconds after a hard tap. Set aside the mussels while you prepare the broth.

2. Heat the vegetable oil in a large saucepan over medium-high heat until shimmering. Add the shishitos and cook until fragrant and just beginning to brown, about 1 minute. Add the ginger and garlic and cook for another minute.

3. Whisk in the broth, followed by the miso, followed by the fish sauce, brown sugar and finally the beer. Bring to a simmer, then add the mussels. Cover and cook for 1 to 2 minutes, until most of the mussels have opened.

4. Stir in the harissa and juice from 2 limes.

5. Turn out into a large bowl and finish with the cilantro. Serve with the lime quarters, the cooking broth and some crusty bread.

Note: If you have any broth left over, freeze it and use it in the next batch.

Bourbon Bread Pudding

FEEDS 6 TO 8

3 ounces dried cherries, blueberries, and/or raisins (about ½ cup), chopped

3 ounces bourbon **B**

1 teaspoon unsalted butter, at room temperature

12 ounces cubed bread, such as challah, French or focaccia

4 large eggs, separated

⅓ cup plus 1 tablespoon sugar

2 cups whole milk

1 cup heavy cream

1 teaspoon freshly grated nutmeg **P**

Bread pudding is one of my favorite desserts because it delivers such a depth of flavor and a range of textures, with its custardy interior and crusty and slightly chewy outer crust. In order to develop that, you really need the bread to absorb all the dairy . . . so don't skimp on the soak time. As for the bourbon . . . no explanation required, but if you don't have bourbon, just about any good whiskey (or whisky) will do. Try a spiced rum **B** sometime.

1. Heat the oven to 350°F.

2. Combine the dried fruit and bourbon in a large bowl and set aside.

3. Coat a 1½-quart round baking dish with the butter, add the bread to the dish and set aside.

4. Beat the egg yolks and ⅓ cup of the sugar in a stand mixer fitted with the paddle attachment until the yolks lighten in color and the sugar is completely dissolved.* Stir into the fruit-bourbon mixture. Add the milk, cream and nutmeg. Set aside.

5. Load up your mixer's whisk attachment and beat the egg whites to soft peaks. With the mixer still running, gradually add the remaining 1 tablespoon sugar and beat until stiff peaks form. Fold the whipped egg whites into the custard mixture, being sure to remove about 2 cups for you to drink as the pudding bakes. Pour the remainder over the bread, pushing the bread down into the liquid and allowing it to soak for 20 minutes before baking.

6. Bake for 35 to 40 minutes, until golden brown on top and the interior hits 190°F. Remove from the oven and cool for 10 minutes before serving.

* This could also be accomplished with an electric hand mixer or even a whisk if you've got the arm for it. (Actually, it's all in the wrist.)

Bad Day Bitter Martini

SERVES 1

2 cups ice cubes

2½ ounces London dry gin, such as Beefeater 24 **B**

½ ounce Amaro Montenegro **B**

Grapefruit peel

I am a great lover of martinis, but the classic varieties lack the bitterness I crave; here I out vermouth for amaro. My favorite gin to use is infused with grapefruit so I use the peel of the fruit instead of an olive. For a dirty martini—add a squeeze of grapefruit juice.

General note regarding vodka- and gin-based drinks: Because I want to have the option of having my drinks strong, I tend to keep both gin and vodka in the freezer (along with cocktail glasses). This means I don't have to shake all my drinks with ice. That said, sometimes you want to mix with ice, either to emulsify/aerate or to allow the melting ice to soften the drink a bit. In this case, the two spirits involved are of different viscosity, so I find a quick stir does the trick.

1. Wrap the ice cubes up in a clean towel and smack it against the counter a few times to crush.* Fill a martini glass with 1 cup of the crushed ice. Add the remaining 1 cup of crushed ice to the bottom of a Boston-style cocktail shaker **H**.

2. Add the gin and Amaro Montenegro and stir until chilled, about 15 seconds. Discard the ice from the martini glass and strain the gin mixture into the serving glass. Garnish with grapefruit peel and serve immediately.

* At the end of a hard day, this action in and of itself is quite refreshing.

Char-Burgers

1 pound boneless, skinless
   Arctic char fillets
⅓ cup panko bread crumbs
¼ cup finely diced scallions
¼ cup finely diced red bell pepper
1 teaspoon prepared horseradish
1 large egg white
2 teaspoons wasabi fumi furikake **P**
1 teaspoon kosher salt
¼ teaspoon freshly ground black
   pepper
2 tablespoons vegetable oil
4 onion rolls
Kewpie mayonnaise* (optional),
   for serving

Everybody loves a good charbroil burger, right? Well, I love a good char-burger; that is, a burger composed of Arctic char, a member of the salmon family that is not only darned good for you (omega fatty acids . . . you can never have too many), but sustainable as well.

1. If the char is frozen, thaw at room temp for about 30 minutes before chopping. If it's raw, freeze for 30 minutes first. Chop the char into ¼-inch cubes and transfer to a medium mixing bowl.

2. Fold in the panko, scallions, bell pepper, horseradish, egg white, fumi furikake, salt and pepper.

3. Divide the mixture into 4 equal portions and shape into ¾-inch-thick patties. Cover and refrigerate for 30 minutes.

4. Heat the vegetable oil in a 12-inch cast-iron pan **H** **M** over medium-high heat until it shimmers. Add the burgers to the pan and cook for 4 minutes, or until lightly browned. Flip and cook for another 3 to 4 minutes, until lightly browned and the burger has reached an internal temperature of 135°F.

5. Move the patties to a plate and let rest for 3 minutes before serving on onion rolls and with a good squeeze of mayonnaise.

Note: By the way, this is my favorite dish in this book . . . just so you know.

* A Japanese version of mayo that includes MSG and rice wine vinegar. Its distinctive squeeze bottle is all but ubiquitous in Asian markets. If you don't have it, love the mayo you're with.

One Pot Chicken

FEEDS 6

⅓ cup plus 1 teaspoon kosher salt

1 "roaster" chicken in the 4-pound range

2 teaspoons peanut or canola oil

True confession: When it comes to a roast or rotisserie chicken, I don't care a hoot about crisp skin. Sure, I want it flavorful, and golden brown is always nice, but what I'm after is great meat. Freak? I think not. Consider those rotisserie chickens that fly out of megamart deli sections. By the time they get to the parking lot, steam has erased any "crispness" from the equation, and yet Americans probably buy more of them than they do whole raw chickens.

So here is my recipe for roast chicken. I've never done this on television because it rarely creates a "camera perfect" skin, but listen to me . . . it's the best chicken I've ever made. And it may just be the easiest.

1. Dissolve ⅓ cup of the salt in 2 quarts water in a container large enough to hold the chicken. Make sure the bird's cavity is empty and place in the brine, breast-side down. I typically use a straight-sided container to make sure the bird will submerge. Cover and refrigerate for 8 to 12 hours. (I usually do this in the morning after I make coffee so that I can cook it that night.)

2. To cook, place a 4-quart cast-iron Dutch oven **H** **M** in the middle of your actual oven (the one with knobs and buttons on it) and crank the controls to 550°F. This is typically as hot as a residential oven gets unless you file down the lock and set it to "clean," which you never would because it's illegal . . . right?

3. Give the ovens (both of them) at least 30 minutes to get hot. Meanwhile, drain and thoroughly dry the bird with paper towels, allowing it to come to room temp while you wait on the oven.

4. When the oven is good and hot, rub the bird down with the peanut oil and sprinkle on the remaining 1 teaspoon salt, then open the oven door, slide out the rack holding the Dutch oven, remove the lid, and drop the bird straight down into it, breast-side up. Quickly position the rocket-hot lid atop, slide the rack back in, and get the door closed as quickly as possible.

5. Leave the chicken alone for 15 minutes. Then remove the lid and baste the top of the bird with some of the juices that have accumulated at the bottom of the pot. Cook, uncovered, for 12 minutes more. Leave the Dutch oven's lid in the oven to keep it warm for the next step.

6. Remove the Dutch oven to a safe spot (the cooktop would be fine), replace the lid, and don't touch for 10 minutes. Then remove the lid and allow the bird to rest for 5 minutes. At this point you might want to use your instant-read thermometer **H** to take a reading right in the middle of the breast. I usually see 150°F at this point. And yes, that's okay. Carryover will take care of the rest.

7. Slide a pair of tongs **H** or a wooden spoon into the cavity and gently lift the bird out to a platter or carving board, tilting it first so that any hot juices can exit into the pot.

8. I serve this in a rather unorthodox but insanely satisfying manner. Pour the juices (a lovely comingling of schmaltz and jus) into a few bowls and position them around the platter, which should be central on the table. Give everyone a knife (not too long or sharp) and allow them to carve off hunks of bird, which should then be dipped (by hand) into the juices and consumed forthwith. Plates? We don't need no stinkin' plates! But you will need several napkins. You're welcome.

* I know . . . I've gone on the record many times as being anti-baste, but that's when turkey was the critter in question, and turkey ain't chicken. In this case we want to promote browning, and getting some of the fallen fat up top will assist that process . . .

Heavenly Orbs of Belgian Goodness

FEEDS 4 AS A SIDE

1½ pounds fresh Brussels sprouts

3 tablespoons olive oil

kosher salt

½ teaspoon sesame oil

½ teaspoon fish sauce [P]

½ teaspoon red pepper flakes [P]

2 ounces roasted peanuts, chopped

In November 2008, a Swede named Linus Urbanec set the world record, consuming 31 brussels sprouts in one minute. I'm telling you right now . . . I can beat that. These pygmy cabbages are hands down my favorite vegetables and this is my everyday method for cooking them . . . with a variation.

1. Heat the oven to 425°F.

2. Trim the dry ends from the sprouts and remove any yellow outer leaves, then halve the sprouts longitudinally.

3. Coat the sprouts with the olive oil and salt to taste in a large bowl and spread in an even layer on a half-sheet pan, placing the cut sides down. Roast for 20 to 25 minutes or until the sprouts are lightly browned and tender.

4. Toss the warm sprouts with the sesame oil, fish sauce, red pepper flakes and peanuts. Serve warm.

Bacon Maple Sprouts

FEEDS 4 AS A SIDE

4 rashers bacon

1½ pounds Brussels sprouts

1 large apple, chopped

2 tablespoons Dijon mustard

1 tablespoon maple syrup

Nothing complements the flavor (and counteracts the health benefits) of Brussels sprouts quite like salty pig candy.

1. Heat the oven to 350°F.

2. Place the bacon on a half sheet pan and roast for 20 minutes, flipping once, until crisp. Remove the pan from the oven and the bacon from the pan.

3. While the bacon is making the kitchen smell awesome, trim and split the sprouts as described in step 2 of Heavenly Orbs of Belgian Goodness.

4. Toss the sprouts and apples with the bacon fat and spread into an even layer on a half sheet pan, placing as many sprouts cut-side down as possible.

5. Roast for 20 to 25 minutes, until the sprouts are browned and tender. Crumble the bacon while the sprouts roast.

6. Meanwhile, whisk together the mustard and syrup. When the sprouts and apples are brown, put them back in the bowl you seasoned them in and toss with the maple mustard and bacon.

Weeknight Spaghetti

FEEDS 2

I remember sneaking into the theater to see *The Godfather* when it first came out, and it taught me a few valuable lessons.

1. Horses are messy.
2. Whatever cannoli are, they're better than guns.
3. When you "go to the mattresses," the best spaghetti sauce you can make is built on canned tomatoes.

Well, I feel like I'm "going to the mattresses" just about every day, so I've Bobby Flay-ed my old recipe for quick assembly.

16 ounces extra-virgin olive oil

6 large garlic cloves, crushed

3 thyme sprigs

2 rosemary sprigs

10 basil leaves, plus more for serving

1 teaspoon red pepper flakes [P]

1 28-ounce can whole San Marzano tomatoes, drained

1 teaspoon kosher salt

1 or 2 white anchovies [P]

½ pound dry spaghetti

1 tablespoon kosher salt

2 tablespoons (¼ stick) unsalted butter

Parmesan cheese

1. Combine the olive oil, garlic, thyme, rosemary, basil and red pepper flakes in a narrow saucepan over medium heat. As the heat builds, there will be considerable bubbling as the water cooks out of the garlic and herbs. When this dies down and the basil and garlic turn brown, kill the heat and let the mixture steep until cool. Strain the oil into a jar and toss the solids. Use immediately or cover tightly and freeze for later use.

2. Heat 3 tablespoons of the herb oil in a wide sauté pan over medium heat. Add the tomatoes and salt to the pan, and cook for 5 to 7 minutes, breaking up the tomatoes as they soften, using a wooden spatula or an old school potato masher.

3. Reduce the heat, stir in the anchovies, and cook for another 5 minutes, or until the anchovies completely vanish from view.

4. Meanwhile, cook the pasta using the Cold Water Pasta Method [M].

5. Fish the spaghetti out of the water with tongs [H] or a hand strainer, allowing most but not all the water to drain away. Stir the pasta into the sauce and cook on low for 5 minutes. Finish with the butter, Parmesan and fresh basil. If the sauce seems too dry, add ¼ cup of the pasta water and serve.

I served for several years as the culinary commentator on a TV program called *Iron Chef America*. One of the Iron Chefs, a guy named Bobby Flay, started pretty much every battle by having one of his sous-chefs make up batches of herb and chile oils. Smart move, because if you have a good flavored oil around, you can basically start a lot of dishes in medias res.

The U.S. government considers herbal oils, especially those containing garlic, to be potentially dangerous because the anaerobic environment provided can support the growth of the microbial nasty that causes botulism. The heat of cooking will kill the nasties, but any spores they produce are heat resistant. The freezer is your best bet for keeping the oil stable for up to 2 months.

Starchy pasta water is the perfect liquid for adjusting pasta sauces at the last minute. I don't know a single chef who throws this magical elixir down the drain until the night is over.

Cream Whipper Chocolate Mousse

FEEDS 4 AS DESSERT

8 ounces 54 percent bittersweet
    chocolate, finely chopped
4 ounces strong coffee, at room
    temperature
4 ounces water
1½ ounces sugar

SPECIAL EQUIPMENT

1 liter whipped cream siphon **H**
One N_2O charger cartridge

1. Combine a few handfuls of ice cubes with a couple quarts of water in a large bowl and set aside.

2. Add enough water to a 10-inch straight-sided sauté pan to come 1 inch up the side and bring to a bare simmer over medium heat. Combine the chocolate, coffee, water and sugar in a medium metal bowl and set in the simmering water.* Stir occasionally for 4 to 5 minutes, until the chocolate is almost completely melted and the sugar is dissolved.

3. Remove the bowl from the water and set on the ice bath. Whisk for 2 to 3 minutes, or until the mixture drops to 60°F and is the consistency of heavy cream.

4. Load the mixture into the whipper, being mindful of the maximum fill line. Screw on the lid and, following the manufacturer's instructions, charge with one N_2O cartridge. After you hear the gas discharge, shake vertically 15 to 20 times, then set aside for 1 minute.

5. To serve (into cocktail glasses, of course), invert and slowly squeeze the trigger to dispense.

* Chocolate is often melted in a double-boiler rig, that is, a bowl suspended over boiling water so that steam alone heats the bottom of the pan. This isn't one of those times. Since a considerable amount of liquid has already been added to the chocolate, you can be a bit more aggressive, thermally speaking, and let the bowl touch the water.

Garam Masalmon Steaks

FEEDS 4

4 1-inch-thick salmon steaks
   (about 12 ounces each)
1 teaspoon cumin seeds
1 teaspoon coriander seeds
1 teaspoon fennel seeds
½ teaspoon dry green peppercorns
Canola oil
Kosher salt

Salmon is one of the best grilling fish on earth because it responds so well to smoke and high heat. This spice mix isn't actually a full-on garam masala, but it's close enough to throw around in the title of the recipe.

By the way, if your grill grate looks more mineral than metal, you need to get after that thing with either a steel brush or a pumice stone or brick, which can take off just about anything. Just make sure to give the grate a good rubdown with a lightly oiled cloth before cooking because pumice dust is a little too crunchy.

1. Prepare the grill by lighting 4 quarts of charcoal (one starter chimney's worth **M**) or turning a gas grill to medium-high.

2. Examine the steaks for pin bones by rubbing your fingers lightly over the surface of the meat and use a clean pair of needle-nose pliers to remove them.   Using a sharp paring or boning knife, trim the backbone from the inside of the steak, then trim the stomach flaps of each steak so that one side is missing about 2 inches of skin and the other, 1 inch of meat. Roll the skinless section up into the hollow cavity, then wrap the flap of skin around the outside to form a round resembling a filet mignon. Tie in place with two passes of butcher's twine. Do not tie it too tight or the fish will pop out during cooking.

3. Combine the cumin, coriander, fennel and peppercorns on a double thickness of heavy-duty aluminum foil **H** and toast over the charcoal starter, shaking gently with tongs **H** until the seeds become fragrant. Cool briefly, then coarsely grind in a blade-style electric coffee grinder.

4. Coat the steaks lightly with canola oil, season with a sprinkling of salt, then liberally sprinkle the toasted spice mixture on both sides of the steaks.

5. When the charcoal is completely lit, move it from the starter to the grill grate and pile so the coals cover an area about 13 by 9 inches. Place the cooking grate over for several minutes to heat, then quickly wipe with a rolled dish towel or paper towels (held with tongs) dipped into a bit of cooking oil.

6. Grill the fish to medium-rare, about 3 minutes per side. Keep the grill lid closed and do not move the fish more than once during the process. The fish should be well colored on the outside and barely translucent at the center.

* At least once a year I put my grill grates in my oven and put them through a "self-clean" cycle. This works well with steel or iron. If you've got nonstick grates, you have some serious self-examination to do.

** I keep a pair of stainless steel (food-grade) pliers around for this **H**. Oh, and make sure you pull with the grain of the meat.

Pumpkin Cheesecake

FEEDS 12

This procedure is all about bringing the temperature of the custard up slowly so that the texture will be smooth. Since water can absorb a lot of heat without actually increasing in temperature, it (and the towel) provides considerable thermal cushioning. Also, when exiting the oven, the center should still be a bit wobbly. If it's completely set, it's gonna crack like the San Andreas Fault when it cools.

15 ounces canned pumpkin puree

1 teaspoon ground ginger

1 teaspoon freshly grated nutmeg P

6 ounces plus 1 tablespoon packed dark brown sugar

7 ounces gingersnap cookies

¼ teaspoon kosher salt

2 ounces (½ stick) unsalted butter, melted

3 large eggs

1 tablespoon vanilla extract

16 ounces cream cheese, at room temperature

SPECIAL EQUIPMENT

Electric kettle H

1. Bring the pumpkin puree to a simmer over medium heat in a 2-quart pot and stir occasionally for 2 to 3 minutes, until slightly thickened. Remove from the heat and stir in the ginger, nutmeg and 6 ounces of the brown sugar. Set aside for about 1 hour.

2. Heat the oven to 300°F. Cut a parchment paper circle and long strip to fit the bottom and sides of a 9 x 3-inch round cake pan. Spray the inside of the pan with nonstick cooking spray, then stick the parchment pieces to the bottom and sides.

3. Spin the cookies, the remaining 1 tablespoon brown sugar and the salt in a food processor to fine crumbs. Drizzle the butter in while pulsing to combine. Transfer to the prepped pan and use the bottom of a 1-cup measuring cup or a water glass to uniformly tamp the cookie mixture into place.

4. Bake for 15 minutes, then remove and cool for at least 10 minutes. Meanwhile, bring 2 quarts water to a boil in an electric kettle. Position a rack in the middle of the oven and crank the heat to 300°F.

5. Whisk the eggs and vanilla together in a small mixing bowl and set aside.

6. Beat the cream cheese in a stand mixer fitted with the paddle attachment on low speed for 10 seconds. Add the cooled pumpkin mixture and mix for 30 seconds. Stop and scrape down the sides of the bowl, then crank the speed to medium and beat until the mixture is lump-free.

7. Reduce the speed to low and slowly incorporate the egg mixture, stopping to scrape down the sides of the bowl as needed. Mix for 1 minute or so more to make sure the mixture is uniform and smooth.

8. Lay a kitchen towel in the bottom of a roasting pan and position the cake pan in the center of it. Pour in the batter, then place the roasting pan on the oven rack.

Finally, carefully pour the boiling water into the roasting pan, being careful to avoid getting any in the cake.

9. Bake for 2 hours. Turn the oven off and open the door for 1 minute, then close the door for 30 minutes.

10. Remove the cheesecake from the water bath and refrigerate for 6 hours to completely cool before serving. Do not attempt to remove the water bath from the oven with the cheesecake in it, unless you like water in your cheesecake.

11. To serve, place the cake pan into hot water for a few seconds, then run a small knife or metal spatula around the inner perimeter to free the parchment. Place a piece of parchment paper atop the cake and top with a large plate. Flip the cheesecake over and lift the pan off. Peel away the parchment and place a cardboard cake circle or large plate on the bottom of the cake and flip the whole thing over again so that it's right side up. Remove any remaining parchment paper and you're good to go.

12. To slice, before cutting, warm a long, thin knife over a low flame or in a glass of hot water; wipe it clean after every cut. I typically go for 12 slices. Store in the fridge, covered, for up to 1 week.

Salisbury Steak

FEEDS 4

Salisbury steak is actually named after one J. H. Salisbury, an English physician who prescribed beef back in the nineteenth century the way some doctors dose out Lipitor today. Although the classic is baked, my version is braised and served in a pan sauce enriched with my secret weapon: milk powder.

1. Whisk the flour and milk powder together in a small bowl.

2. Divide the beef into 4 oval patties approximately 3 x 4 inches. Season both sides with the salt and dredge in the flour mixture. Set on a rack and set aside at room temp.*

3. Heat a large heavy sauté pan over medium-high heat and sauté the diced onion in 2 teaspoons of the clarified butter. When the onion is brown and soft, invite the mushrooms to the pan and cook until the mushrooms brown and reduce by half.

4. Transfer the mushroom mixture to a plate and add the remaining 1 tablespoon clarified butter to the pan. Once melted, add the patties and cook for 4 minutes on the first side.

5. Meanwhile, whisk together the milk, red wine and beef flavor packet in a separate bowl.

6. Flip the patties and cook for 2 minutes on the second side. Add the mushroom mixture back to the pan, distributing it evenly around the beef patties.

7. Pour in the milk mixture, cover, reduce the heat to medium and simmer for 10 minutes to thicken the sauce.

⅓ cup all-purpose flour

2 tablespoons nonfat dry milk powder

1 pound ground sirloin, dry aged if possible

½ teaspoon kosher salt

1 yellow onion, diced

2 teaspoons plus 1 tablespoon Clarified Butter M

1 pint button mushrooms, stemmed and sliced

⅔ cup low-fat milk

⅓ cup red wine

1 beef ramen flavor packet

***** This is to keep the surface of the meat as dry as possible.

Snapper-Dome

FEEDS 4 AS AN ENTREE

"One fish enters, four meals leave."

2 lemons, very thinly sliced

6 fresh flat-leaf parsley sprigs

1 1- to 2-pound whole yellow or
    vermillion snapper, cleaned and
    trimmed

3 pounds kosher salt

3 large egg whites

1. Heat the oven to 450°F. Line a half sheet pan with parchment paper.

2. Place a few lemon slices and the parsley sprigs inside the cavity of the fish.

3. Combine the salt, egg whites and ¼ cup water in a large mixing bowl, working it together with your hands until it resembles wet sand and holds together when squeezed. Place about a third of the salt mixture on the sheet pan and shape it into an oval roughly the size of the fish and ½ inch thick. Lay a few lemon slices across the salt and park the fish on top.

4. Pile the remaining salt mixture onto the fish, patting it into a dome ½ inch thick. The end of the tail should stick out of the end of the dome. (Depending on the size of the fish, you may not need all of the salt mixture.)

5. Roast for 15 to 20 minutes, until the dome is lightly browned and the fish reaches an internal temperature of 130°F. How will you know? Because you'll jab your instant-read thermometer **H** right through the dome, that's how.

6. Remove from the oven and let rest for 10 minutes.

7. Use a small hammer, meat tenderizer, mallet or rolling pin to crack the dome. The salt should come off easily in a few large slabs. Use a basting brush to brush any excess salt off the fish.

8. Use a fish knife or serrated pie server to make an incision all the way down the back of the fish and around the gill plate. Lift off the skin, working from head to tail.

9. Remove the fillet in pieces from the top side of the fish. Once the top fillet is removed, gently remove the bone by pulling the tail up and forward. Remove the bottom fillet below, leaving the skin behind.

Smoky Tequila Sour

SERVES 1

2 limes
1 ounce 100 percent agave silver
  or blanco tequila **B**
1 ounce Amaro Montenegro **B**
½ small orange, juiced
  (about 1½ ounces)
1 tablespoon light agave nectar[**]
1 dash liquid smoke **P**

Sours are a classic cocktail family that includes the whiskey sour and the margarita. All sours call for a spirit, citrus and a sweetener. This one adds bitterness and smoke.[*] The drying sensation that lingers on the tongue after consuming something bitter leaves me wanting more. Amaro Montenegro is an Italian digestif, light and slightly bitter with a hint of orange.

1. Fill an old-fashioned glass with ice and set aside.

2. Cut a wedge from 1 of the limes and reserve, then juice both limes (you should get about 2 ounces) into the bottom of a Boston-style cocktail shaker **H**. Add the tequila, Amaro Montenegro, orange juice, agave nectar and half a dozen or so ice cubes. Cover and shake for 30 seconds.

3. Strain the mixture through a cocktail strainer into the prepared glass. Add the liquid smoke, garnish with the lime wedge and serve immediately.

[*] I realize that many mezcals deliver smokiness, but I want to be able to mix with a tequila blanco, which is typically devoid of such complexity.

[**] If you're going to sweeten a tequila drink, it makes sense to use a sweetner derived from the same botanical source.

Mushroom Stroganoff

FEEDS 6 TO 8

10 ounces extra wide egg noodles

2 tablespoons (¼ stick) unsalted butter

5 portobello mushrooms, stems and
   gills removed, thinly sliced*

1 teaspoon kosher salt

10 scallions, thinly sliced on the bias,
   white bottoms and green tops
   separated**

1 tablespoon all-purpose flour

14 ounces beef broth

1 cup sour cream

4 ounces goat cheese

½ teaspoon freshly ground black
   pepper, plus more for serving

When I was growing up, beef stroganoff was my jam. My mom's version was solid, but over the years I became suspicious of the beef. I'm just not convinced it's at home in this dish. After all, Russians eat noodles, sour cream is practically their national condiment and both Tolstoy and Chekhov wrote about mushrooms. I rest my case.

1. Add the noodles to 4 quarts cold water in a large pot, cover, and place over high heat. Cook to al dente, 18 to 22 minutes, stirring occasionally (Cold Water Pasta, see M).

2. Melt 1 tablespoon of the butter in a 10-inch straight-sided sauté pan over medium-high heat.

3. Increase the heat to high, add half of the mushrooms and sprinkle with ½ teaspoon of the salt. Sauté for 5 to 6 minutes, until the mushrooms darken and reduce in volume by half. Remove to a bowl.***

4. Repeat with the remaining 1 tablespoon butter, the remaining mushrooms and the remaining ½ teaspoon salt, along with the white bottoms of the scallions.

5. Return the first batch of mushrooms to the pan, sprinkle in the flour and stir to combine, cooking for 1 minute, or until the flour disappears and a dark "fond" appears on the bottom of the pan.

6. Deglaze the pan with the beef broth and as soon as it simmers (almost immediately), decrease the heat to low and cook for 10 to 12 minutes to reduce the liquid.

7. Add the sour cream, goat cheese and pepper and stir to combine. Bring to a bare simmer and cook, covered, for 2 to 4 minutes.

8. Drain the noodles and stir gently into the mushroom mixture. Turn onto a platter and garnish with the scallion tops and additional pepper.

* The portobello is nothing but an overgrown cremini mushroom. The name was devised as a marketing ploy in the early 1980s.

** I think scallions are way underutilized in the American kitchen. You just need to remember to toss the top inch or so because it's typically too fibrous and dry. Also always cut on the bias. If you cut straight across, you get rounds that roll off the cutting board!

*** If the pan is really hot, when you toss the mushrooms they'll make a funny hissing sound, kind of like they're singing . . . or screaming, which I guess makes more sense.

Turkey Tikka Masala

FEEDS 4

2 teaspoons coriander seeds
1½ teaspoons black peppercorns
1 teaspoon cumin seeds
¼ teaspoon brown mustard seeds
2 whole cloves
½ teaspoon cardamom pods
¼ teaspoon ground cinnamon
⅛ teaspoon red pepper flakes **P**
⅛ teaspoon freshly grated nutmeg **P**
2 teaspoons kosher salt
1½ pounds boneless, skinless
  turkey thighs
1 cup plain whole-milk yogurt
¼ cup canola oil
1 large onion, chopped
4 garlic cloves, grated on a rasp
  grater **H**
2 tablespoons grated fresh ginger
2 small fresh red chiles, such as Fresno
  or cayenne, seeded and minced
1 28-ounce can diced tomatoes
1 cup coconut milk
1 tablespoon fresh lime juice
Cooked basmati rice, for serving
Fresh mint or cilantro leaves,
  for serving

There ought to be a name for dishes that everyone thinks are from one place but are actually from another . . . something like "*malageoism*" or some such. Chicken tikka masala would certainly be a poster food for *malageoism* because here in the United States everyone thinks it's "Indian" food when it's 100 percent British. Of course, it wouldn't have happened if England hadn't soaked up the culture of the subcontinent during the days of the Raj. Well, I'm putting a distinctly North American spin on it by replacing the chicken with an American bird named after Turkey. Namely . . . turkey. It may be a postcolonial double *malageoism*, but it's damned tasty.

1. Combine the coriander seeds, peppercorns, cumin seeds, mustard seeds and cloves in an 8-inch cast-iron skillet **H** **M** over medium-high heat and toast, moving the pan constantly, until you can smell the cumin, 3 to 4 minutes. Remove the mixture from the hot pan and cool on a plate for 5 minutes. Grind the mixture, along with the cardamom, cinnamon, red pepper flakes and nutmeg, in a spice grinder for 1 minute.

2. Transfer half of the spice mixture, 1 teaspoon of the salt, and the turkey to a 1-gallon resealable bag. Seal the bag and shake to coat the turkey in the spice mixture. Add the yogurt to the bag and "squish" to coat. Refrigerate the bag for 30 minutes.

3. Meanwhile, heat the canola oil in a 12-inch straight-sided sauté pan over medium-high until it shimmers. Add the onion and the remaining 1 teaspoon salt and cook until the onion is browned around the edges, 11 to 12 minutes, stirring occasionally.

4. Reduce the heat to low and add the garlic, ginger and chiles. Cook, stirring constantly, until the onion has softened and browned completely, 7 to 8 minutes more. Add the remaining half of the spice mixture and the tomatoes. Cook, stirring occasionally, until reduced and darkened in color, 15 to 20 minutes.

5. Heat your grill (gas, charcoal **M**, doesn't matter) to high.

6. Remove the turkey from the yogurt mixture, keeping as much yogurt on the meat as possible. Grill the turkey until the yogurt is charred, about 5 minutes per side. Rest the turkey for 5 minutes and trash the remaining yogurt mix still in the bag.

7. Chop the turkey into bite-size pieces. Add the turkey, coconut milk and lime juice to the tomato mixture; stir to combine and heat through.

8. Serve over basmati rice with fresh mint or cilantro.

Note: If you really don't want to mess with your grill for the turkey, I'm not going to judge. You could use a grill pan or even a cast-iron skillet, but you need to get it really, really hot. Me, I'd rather crank up the grill. Look at it this way, you could make the whole dish on your grill. Just a thought.

Totally Panini-Pressed Dinner

FEEDS 1

I am totally in love with my panini press, a heavy-duty thing made by Krups. I don't think I've ever made an actual panini, but I have made just about everything else, including this deceptively simple dish that can be served as a side (nice with steak) or as a meal all on its own.

3 rashers thick-cut bacon

1 small red onion, frenched **M**

1 pint cremini mushrooms, sliced
 ¼ inch thick

2 ounces baby spinach

1 teaspoon buffalo wing sauce

SPECIAL EQUIPMENT

Panini press **H**

1. Place the bacon in a panini press, close the lid and heat to high. Cook the bacon until crisp, 7 to 8 minutes. Remove the bacon to a paper towel–lined plate.

2. Add the red onion, close the lid and cook for 4 minutes. Remove to a mixing bowl.

3. Add the mushrooms in a single layer, close the lid and cook for 2 minutes. Meanwhile, crumble the bacon into the bowl with the onion. Remove the mushrooms from the press and add to the bowl.

4. Add the spinach, close the lid and cook for 30 seconds. Transfer the spinach to the bowl.

5. Drizzle on the buffalo wing sauce. Toss and serve.

Grilled Squid Salad

FEEDS 6

2 pounds whole squid, cleaned,
   or 1½ pounds precleaned
1 teaspoon plus 1 tablespoon olive oil
1½ teaspoons kosher salt
1 teaspoon freshly ground black
   pepper
½ teaspoon ground sumac **P**
½ teaspoon ground cumin
½ cup julienned red onion
3 ounces kale, cut into ribbons
   (chiffonade)
1 cup cooked farro
⅓ cup chopped kalamata olives
1 small tomato, coarsely chopped
1 tablespoon red wine vinegar

Here are some simple facts to consider: *Loligo opalescens,* or California market squid, which makes up a vast majority of the squid in American markets, is high in protein, low in fat, and extremely plentiful. I personally suspect it to be of alien origin and probably just increasing its numbers until the giant squid, along with the velociraptors of the sea, the Humboldt squid, rise up and press humankind into slavery. What can we do? Eat as many of them as possible. It's your duty to mankind.

1. Set a cooling rack on one side of a grill and heat the grill to high.

2. To clean the whole squid, grip the squid body, or "mantle," in one hand and the head with the tentacles in the other. Gently pull the head away from the mantle. Most of the innards will stay attached to the head and will be pulled out of the body. Pull out the clear, feather-shaped backbone, or "quill." Cut off the tentacles just above the eyes, remove the pea-shaped beak and innards, and discard. Remove the skin by grabbing with a paper towel and pulling away from the body; discard.

3. Place the cleaned squid in a mixing bowl with 1 teaspoon of the olive oil, 1 teaspoon of the salt, the pepper, sumac and cumin. Set aside.

4. Set the red onion in a large mixing bowl.

5. Place the squid tentacles on the cooling rack and the tubes directly on the grill grate and grill for 1½ to 2 minutes. Flip and cook for another 1½ minutes. Be careful not to overcook.

6. Immediately chop the tentacles and tubes into bite-size pieces and add to the bowl of onion. Top with the kale and let rest for 2 minutes. Toss to combine while still warm so the squid helps to slightly wilt the kale.

7. Add the remaining 1 tablespoon olive oil, the farro, olives, tomato, vinegar and the remaining ½ teaspoon salt and toss to combine. Serve warm or at room temperature.

ANYTIME

Peach Punch Pops

MAKES 16 POPS

I love Popsicles and I love cocktails. I love peaches. I love bourbon and I love iced tea. So this is pretty much a no-brainer. Just make sure you don't mix these up with the ones you give the kids. Of course, if one of the little boogers does swipe one, the cayenne will teach them a lesson!

8 peaches, pitted and cubed
2 cups iced tea
¼ cup sugar
8 ounces bourbon **P**
Pinch of kosher salt
Tiny pinch of cayenne pepper

SPECIAL EQUIPMENT

Popsicle molds, Popsicle sticks

1. Blend the peaches, tea, sugar, bourbon, salt and cayenne in a blender until smooth. Transfer to the fridge and chill for about 4 hours.

2. Pour the peach mixture into Popsicle molds, add a stick and freeze for 4 hours, or until solid. Store in a zip-top bag in the freezer for up to 2 weeks.

* In the South, we would refer to this as "sweetea," that is, black tea that has been liberally sweetened while it was still hot.

The General's Fried Chicken

8 pieces chicken (about 4 pounds—
preferably 4 legs and 4 thighs)

3 tablespoons kosher salt

2 teaspoons freshly ground
black pepper

2 teaspoons ground sumac **P**

1 teaspoon cayenne pepper

1 teaspoon garlic powder

2 cups all-purpose flour

2 tablespoons cornstarch

1 cup buttermilk

1 large egg

2 tablespoons bourbon **B**

2 quarts peanut oil

Why "General's"? Because a general is better than a colonel, that's why. (Drops spoon, walks out of kitchen.)

1. Place the chicken pieces on a cooling rack set over a half sheet pan and sprinkle with the salt. Set aside at room temp for 30 minutes.

2. Meanwhile, combine the black pepper, sumac, cayenne and garlic powder in a small bowl, then divide the blend into two equal portions (total mixture = 8 teaspoons). Sprinkle half of the said mixture on the chicken and refrigerate, uncovered, for at least 4 hours or overnight.

3. Remove the chicken from the refrigerator 30 minutes before cooking. Whisk together the flour, cornstarch and the remaining spice mixture in a large bowl. In another bowl, whisk together the buttermilk, egg and bourbon.

4. Dunk the chicken pieces, one at a time, into the buttermilk mixture, then dredge in the flour mixture (don't worry about letting any excess buttermilk drain off the chicken first). After shaking in the dredge container to coat, use your fingers to massage the flour coating onto the chicken. **

5. Remove the coated chicken to the cooling rack set inside a half sheet pan and set aside for at least 10 minutes or up to an hour. When time's almost up, heat the peanut oil to 350°F in a large Dutch oven over medium-high heat, about 15 minutes. (See Fry Station Setup, **M**.)

6. Fry the chicken in three batches, rotating the pieces every 3 to 4 minutes and adjusting the heat as needed to maintain 325°F. If you manage the heat just right, the exterior of the chicken will be golden brown right as the interior temperature hits 155°F, 12 to 15 minutes per batch. Set the chicken onto a paper towel–lined pan to cool for at least 5 minutes before serving.

＊ I'm not a fan of fried breast meat, but if you must, make sure that the rib cage is still in place and that the entire wing has been removed.

＊＊ My director of culinary ops, Meghan, uses *tszuj* (pronounced "jujj") to describe this process. It's not in any dictionary that I can find, but according to the Interwebs, it's got to do with kind of squeezing hair or fabric in the hand, so I'll allow it.

Preserved Lemons-ade

MAKES 2 CUPS

1 cup Quick Preserved Lemons
    (recipe follows)
½ cup sugar
½ cup water
½ cup fresh lemon juice
Soda water, for serving

I've always loved lemonade, but generally it's just sweet and tart; there's not a lot going on beneath the surface. By using preserved lemons, all that changes. There's real depth of flavor here, and the bit of salt that comes across balances the sweetness and mingles with the fizz. And yes, you could pour some vodka in there . . . free country.

1. Combine the preserved lemons, sugar and water in a small saucepan. Bring to a simmer over medium heat and cook until the sugar dissolves, about 1 minute. Cool the lemon syrup off the heat for 1 hour. Add the lemon juice and stir to combine.

2. To serve, pour 2 ounces of the lemon syrup over ice and top with 4 ounces soda water.

Quick Preserved Lemons

Makes 1 pint

4 medium lemons, scrubbed
    and dried
¼ cup coarse sea salt
Juice of 1 lemon

I'm a huge lemonhead, and to my mouth's mind nothing delivers the essence of lemon quite like preserved lemons. They're a staple in Middle Eastern and Moroccan cuisine, but honestly, anytime a savory recipe calls for lemon, I reach for these. Just make sure you rinse them off before you use them.

1. Remove the top and tail from each lemon.

2. Slice each lemon into 8 wedges, removing any seeds as you go. Reserve as much of the juice as possible.

3. Layer the sliced lemons in a clean wide-mouthed jar—sprinkling with the salt at each layer. Don't be shy with the salt—you'll rinse it off later. Pack the jar as tightly as possible.

4. Top the jar with any remaining lemon juice, leaving about ¼ inch of head space in the jar.

5. Stash in the refrigerator for 4 days, then flip the bottle over and age another 4 days before sampling. The peel should be nice and soft. This can be used immediately or kept in the fridge for up to 3 months.

6. Rinse the lemons before eating. Preserved lemons are a welcome addition to creamy pasta dishes, grain salads, braises, grilled fish . . . heck, even vanilla ice cream. Be aware that many recipes call for the pulp to be discarded because most of the flavor is in the peel itself.

Pâté de Sardine

I adore canned sardines. In fact, I'd say I am a connoisseur of the form, with favorite brands from the United States, France, Portugal and Spain. I enjoy them right out of the can most of the time, but this pâté is my absolute favorite way to consume them.

If you happen to drop by my place for hors d'oeuvres, odds are I'll serve this stuff with thin baguette toasts for dipping. If it's fancy, we'll spread instead.

270

2 cans oil-packed sardines **P** (about 4 ounces each)

2 ounces (½ stick) unsalted butter, at room temperature

1 large shallot, chopped

2 tablespoons fresh lemon juice

3 tablespoons finely chopped fresh herbs, such as chives, parsley or dill

1. Dump the sardines and their oil in the bowl of a food processor, along with the butter, shallot and lemon juice, and process until smooth. Add 2 tablespoons of the herbs and pulse 2 or 3 times.

2. Pack the pâté into a small ramekin (or back into the sardine cans). Smooth with a spatula, then top with the remaining 1 tablespoon herbs. Wrap tightly in plastic wrap and refrigerate for at least 1 hour to firm the texture.

* Tightly wrapped, the pâté will keep for about 5 days. It doesn't freeze well though, so . . . don't do that.

Hot Saltine Hack

MAKES 40 CRACKERS

Some might argue the hacking of an iconic cracker to be culinary blasphemy.

Whatever.

2 tablespoons Clarified Butter M, melted

1 tablespoon hot sauce

1 teaspoon dry mustard powder

1 sleeve saltines (about 40 crackers)

1. Heat the oven to 350°F.

2. Meanwhile, whisk the butter, hot sauce and dry mustard together in a large mixing bowl. Add the saltines and toss to coat.

3. Spread the crackers on a half sheet pan.

4. Bake for 8 to 10 minutes, until the saltines just start to brown.

5. Try warm with the sardine pâté (see page 168).

Salty Chocolaty Peanut Buttery Crunchy Bars

MAKES 120 1-INCH PIECES

16 ounces sugar

12 ounces orange blossom honey

18 ounces creamy peanut butter

12 ounces semisweet chocolate chips

1 teaspoon vegetable shortening

½ teaspoon Maldon salt **P**

Whether you're making ice cream, fudge, caramel or brittle, candy making is all about controlling the temperature and therefore the concentration and crystallization of a sugar syrup. When cooking, the hotter the syrup, the more concentrated it is and, typically, the harder the candy will be—295°F is a kind of magical thermal way point. Any lower and the candy will be really chewy, any higher and it'll crack your teeth like brittle. But 295°F . . . magic.

1. Line a half sheet pan with a silicone baking mat or a piece of parchment paper coated with nonstick cooking spray. Combine the sugar, honey and ½ cup water in a 4-quart saucepan, and bring to a boil over medium heat. Cover and boil for 5 minutes.

2. Put the peanut butter in a large heatproof bowl and have standing by on a clean kitchen towel or no-skid pad.

3. Remove the lid of the saucepan and clip a candy thermometer **H** to the side. When the mixture reaches 295°F, remove from the heat and quickly pour the sugar mixture over the peanut butter and use a wooden spoon to combine.* Don't try for a homogenous mixture. There should still be some streaks of peanut butter throughout.

4. Immediately pour the mixture onto the prepared pan and spread into an even layer. The mixture will begin to harden right away. Use a pizza wheel to cut the candy into 1-inch squares while still warm. Cool completely, about 45 minutes.

5. Add enough water to a large saucepan to come up the sides 1 inch, then bring to a simmer over medium heat. Combine the chocolate and shortening in a medium heatproof bowl and melt over the simmering water, stirring occasionally until completely smooth. Pour over the cooled peanut butter candy and spread into an even layer. Cool for 3 to 4 minutes and then sprinkle with the salt.

6. After the chocolate has set completely, cut the candy again with the pizza wheel, following the lines created by the first cuts. Store in an airtight container for up to 1 week. Or just eat it all right then and there. No one would blame you one bit.

Note: I usually give this stuff away as bribes . . . It's that powerful.

* Why wood? Because metal conducts heat and could result in localized crystallization, throwing off the texture of the finished candies. Although the fat from the peanut butter will likely mitigate this, there's no reason not to play it safe.

Grilled Shishitos

FEEDS 2

½ pound shishito chiles, rinsed
and dried
1 teaspoon olive oil
½ teaspoon kosher salt
2 teaspoons soy sauce
1 ounce katsuobushi flakes **P**
(a handful)

Suddenly, shishitos are everywhere, and I for one couldn't be happier. These mild chiles are crinkly, green, thin-skinned and sweet and probably migrated from Portugal in the sixteenth century to Japan, where they have long been served in izakaya, which is a fancy way of saying they're bar food. Shishito have caught on in the United States, where they are typically panfried or grilled and served with a mound of shaved bonito or katsuobushi on top. Although I usually bag mine at a nearby Japanese market, more and more upscale markets are keeping them on hand.

1. Heat a grill to high.*

2. Toss the shishitos with the olive oil and salt in a large mixing bowl. Arrange the chiles in an even layer on the grill and cook, uncovered, for 3 minutes. Flip and grill for another 2 to 3 minutes, until the skins are slightly blistered.

3. Move the shishitos back to the mixing bowl and toss with the soy sauce. Then quickly place on a platter and top with the katsuobushi flakes.

4. To consume, simply grab one by the stem and eat the entire pod, seeds and all.

Note: According to chile legend, nine out of every ten shishitos are mild . . . that one, though, it's a stinker.

* Charcoal **M** is absolutely the best fuel for this.

Roasted Chile Salsa

MAKES ABOUT 1 QUART

6 Roma tomatoes, halved horizontally

5 jalapeño peppers, halved and seeded

4 large garlic cloves

2 dried ancho chiles **P**, seeded and
   soaked in hot water for 10 minutes*

1 red bell pepper, seeded and quartered

½ red onion, roughly chopped

1 tablespoon olive oil

Juice of 1 lime

1 teaspoon kosher salt

1 teaspoon chili powder

Chopped fresh cilantro, parsley,
   or scallions, but not all three

This is the only salsa I keep on hand year-round. I use it in scrambled eggs, on pizza, and, of course, Chilaquiles! (page 21). I know, five jalapeños sounds like a lot, but don't worry, roasting them under the broiler knocks down the heat considerably.

Oh, and I dip chips into this as well. Forgot about that. Sorry.

1. Place an oven rack in the top position and heat the broiler.

2. Squeeze the tomato halves, reserving the juice and seeds. Set aside 2 tomatoes and 1 jalapeño. Toss the remaining 4 tomatoes and 4 jalapeños with the garlic, chiles, bell pepper, onion and olive oil. Spread the mixture on a half sheet pan.

3. Broil for 20 minutes, stirring every 5 minutes to promote even browning.

4. Transfer the broiled vegetables to a food processor and add the reserved tomatoes, jalapeño, lime juice, salt and chili powder. Pulse several times until the mixture reaches salsa consistency. If the mixture seems too dry, add part or all of the reserved tomato liquid.

5. Leave at room temp or refrigerate for a few hours for the flavors to blend. Top with the herbage of your choice and serve on your favorite hubcap. Or, a bowl if you must.

* To seed, snip the stem end off with scissors and shake out the seeds.

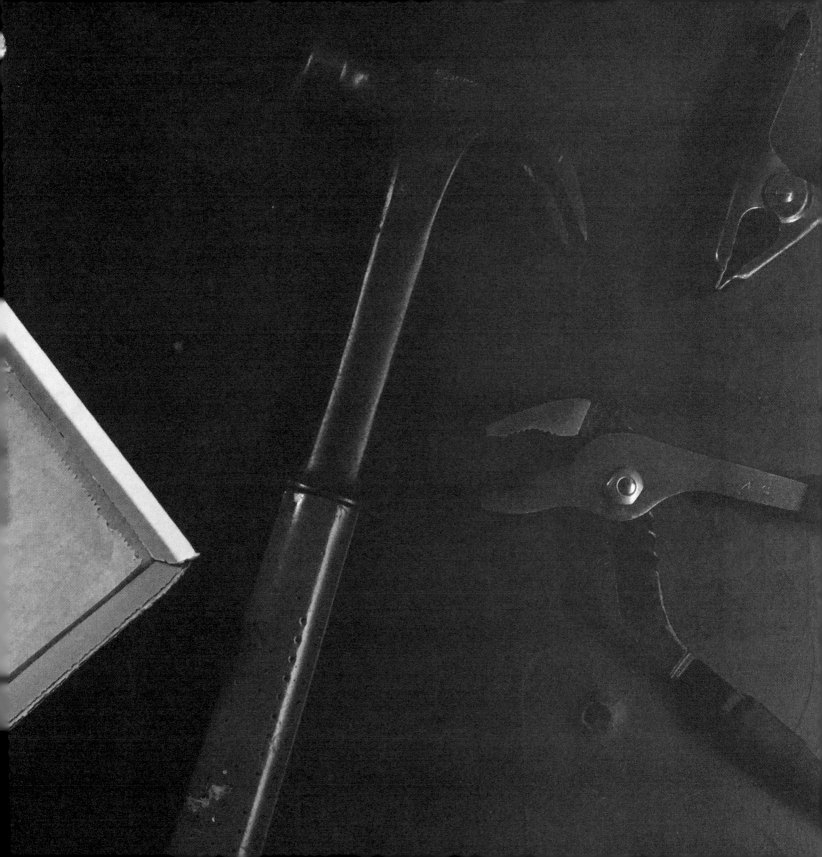

The Last Pizza Dough I'll Ever Need

MAKES 3 10-INCH PIZZAS

690 grams bread flour, plus extra for shaping

9 grams active dry yeast

15 grams sugar

20 grams kosher salt

455 grams bottled water

15 grams olive oil, plus extra for the bowl and crust

SPECIAL EQUIPMENT

Digital scale **H**

Wooden pizza peel (not metal)

Pizza stone

If you happened to catch my live culinary variety show, *The Edible Inevitable Tour*, you know that every night, in more than one hundred cities in the United States, a volunteer and I spun and baked pizzas in my Mighty MegaBake Oven. That meant I needed to come up with a dough that was elastic and plastic, tasty, durable, and easy to make in the tour bus environment. After considerable experimentation I'm pleased to announce that this is indeed the last pizza dough I'll ever need. It might just be the last one you need as well.

1. Place each ingredient into the bowl of a stand mixer in the order listed. Install the dough hook attachment and mix on low until the dough comes together, forming a ball and pulling away from the sides of the bowl. Increase the mixer speed to medium and knead for 5 minutes.

2. Lightly flour the countertop, then round the dough into a smooth ball by folding the edges of the round in toward the center several times and rolling it between your hands on the counter. Lightly oil a bowl and place the dough in the bowl. Cover with plastic wrap and refrigerate for 18 to 24 hours.

3. "Punch down" the dough by turning it out onto a clean countertop and shaping it into a rough rectangle, using your knuckles to work out as many of the large gas bubbles as possible. Then tightly roll the dough into a log 12 to 15 inches long. Cut this into thirds. Shape each third into a disk, then shape the disks into smooth balls. You may want to moisten the counter with water to up the surface tension a bit so that the ball tightens up instead of sliding across the counter.

4. Cover each ball with a clean kitchen towel and set aside for 30 minutes at room temperature. At this point, you can also transfer the dough to airtight plastic containers and refrigerate for up to 8 hours. Just make sure you bring the balls to room temperature 30 minutes before use.

PIZZA TIME

1. Set a pizza stone on the lower rack of the oven (or the floor, if using a gas oven) and crank the heat as high as it will go, hopefully 550°F. Give the oven and the stone a good 30 minutes to heat up.

2. To build the pizza, sprinkle a tablespoon or so of flour on a pizza peel or wooden countertop and place the dough right in the middle. Shape into a disk with the heel of your hand, gently pounding with a circular motion.

3. Use your fingers to form the outer lip, a critical feature that cannot be created with a rolling pin. (In fact, rolling rather than stretching will just ruin the whole gosh-darned thing.)

4. At this point you need to start stretching the dough. The most efficient way is to pass the dough back and forth between your hands, rotating it as you go so that the mass of the dough and gravity work to slowly stretch the gluten.

5. You can also stretch the dough on the board by turning and pulling it, and turning and pulling. If you're working on a peel (which I recommend), jiggle it from time to time to ensure the dough isn't sticking. If it is, shake it loose then lift the edge and add a bit more flour. Keep working the dough until it's almost as wide as your peel (or pan if you need to go that way).

6. Brush the entire dough lightly with olive oil. Ladle an ounce or two of sauce into the middle of the dough then using the back of the ladle, spread it out almost to the edge. Top with fresh herbs (oregano and basil) and a good melting cheese. I usually go with a mixture of mozzarella, Monterery Jack and provolone, but that's me.

7. Slide the pizza onto the hot pizza stone. To do this, position the front edge of the peel about one inch from the back of the stone. Lift the handle and jiggle gently until the pizza slides forward. As soon as the dough touches the stone, start pulling the peel back toward you while still jiggling. While a couple of inches of dough are on the stone, quickly snap the peel straight back. As long as the dough isn't stuck on the peel, it will park itself nicely on the stone.

8. Keep an eye on the dough for the first 3 to 4 minutes. If any big bubbles start ballooning up, reach in with a fork and pop them. Bake for 7 to 10 minutes total or until the top is bubbly and the lip is browned.

9. Slide the peel under the pizza and remove to the counter or a cutting board. Let it rest for at least 2 minutes before slicing with a chef's knife or pizza cutter (one of my favorite multitaskers).

Barley Water

SERVES 8

Despite our health beverage mania (I know a place in L.A. that charges five bucks for lemon water laced with charcoal), Americans still aren't hip to barley water. The Brits have been drinking it at Wimbledon since . . . well, for a long time. Barley is a great source of dietary fiber, which can fight arterial plaque and the rise of LDL cholesterol. It delivers magnesium, which can help control glucose levels, thus providing protection against type 2 diabetes.

Could you just eat more barley? Yes, and you should. But barley water is curiously satisfying and very thirst quenching. So why not drink some too?

2 quarts water
1 cup hulled barley
2 lemons
¼ cup orange blossom honey

1. Combine the water and barley in a medium saucepan, cover and bring to a boil over high heat. Reduce the heat to low and simmer for 30 minutes.

2. While the liquid cooks, peel the lemons with a vegetable peeler, being careful to avoid the bitter white pith. Juice the lemons into a 3-quart pitcher and add the lemon peel.

3. After 30 minutes, strain the barley water through a fine-mesh strainer into the pitcher. Discard the barley. Add the honey and stir to combine. Refrigerate until chilled.

Chuan'r*

1 tablespoon cumin seeds

2 teaspoons fennel seeds

2 teaspoons Sichuan peppercorns P

1 teaspoon garlic powder

1 teaspoon kosher salt

2 pounds lamb shoulder chops or
boneless leg of lamb

SPECIAL EQUIPMENT

16 bamboo skewers

I go through a lot of skewers so I keep a bunch soaking in the fridge at all times. A 12-ounce plastic water bottle makes the perfect vessel. Even full of water, when you open the lid of the bottle, the skewers pop right up. Soak your skewers for at least 30 minutes before grilling.

Big with Beijingers, these cumin-spiced bits of lamb are strung onto skewers and roasted over coals as red as dragons' eyes. I realize cranking up a grill is a bit unusual 'round midnight, but in the summer, when it's hot as blazes well into the evening, it kinda makes sense . . . to me at least.

1. Toast the cumin, fennel and Sichuan peppercorns in a dry skillet over medium heat until fragrant, 1 to 2 minutes. Remove from the pan and let cool. Once cool, grind the spices, the garlic powder and salt in a spice/coffee grinder.

2. Cut the lamb into ½-inch cubes, but don't trim away any of the fat. Sprinkle the cubed meat with half of the spice mixture and thread onto skewers, leaving just enough room at the end to safely handle. Line the skewers up on plastic wrap, roll into a cylinder and refrigerate for at least 1 hour before cooking .

3. Prepare a grill by lighting 4 quarts of charcoal M (1 starter chimney's worth) or turning a gas grill to medium-high. Make sure the grates of the grill are clean and debris free. Quickly wipe the hot grill grate with a towel dipped into a little canola oil, then grill the skewers to medium-rare, about 2 minutes per side. Sprinkle the skewers with more of the spice blend between turns.**

4. It is absolutely imperative that you consume your chuan'r with several cold beers. After all, you're not going anywhere at this hour, right?

* Chuan'r derives from *chuan*, which basically means "threaded on" and is represented by the character 串, which looks like meat on a skewer. How could you not love that?

** If you have a Japanese hibachi or konro-style grill . . . lucky you.

Watermelon Campari Sorbet

MAKES 1 QUART, FEEDS 8

1½ pounds ripe watermelon, cubed
9 ounces sugar
3 tablespoons Campari **B**
1 tablespoon lime zest
2 tablespoons fresh lime juice
¼ teaspoon kosher salt

SPECIAL EQUIPMENT

Ice cream maker

There are plenty of watermelon sorbet recipes that call for vodka. The reason being that alcohol lowers the freezing point (as does sugar), thus ensuring scoopability and a smooth mouthfeel. However, vodka doesn't add zip for flavor, and since cold decreases our ability to taste flavors fully, I figure the melon can use a little help on the complexity front. That's where the Campari comes in with its bitter bite and ever so slight medicinal twang.

1. Puree the watermelon in a blender or food processor. Add the sugar, Campari, lime zest, lime juice and salt, and process for another 30 seconds. Transfer to an airtight container and chill for 1 hour in the refrigerator.

2. Churn according to your ice cream maker's instructions, then return to the airtight container for 3 to 4 hours to harden.

Note: Although the sorbet is delightful on its own, try a small scoop in a champagne glass and top with cold prosecco sometime. That's right . . . a float!

If you don't have a food processor, a decent blender will do just fine. You'll just have to add the watermelon a few chunks at a time.

Cider House Fondue

2 large apples (Honeycrisps are
    perfect), peeled, cored and sliced into
    ⅓-inch rings
200 grams shredded Cheddar cheese
    (New York sharp is my preference)
200 grams Velveeta, cut into chunks
84 ounces half-and-half
42 grams applejack **B**
¼ teaspoon cayenne pepper

SPECIAL EQUIPMENT

Wok **H**
Apple wood chips
Small grill grate

You'll need a stovetop smoker OR a standard wok and a lid for said wok. You could make this out of aluminum foil, but I use the 15½-inch lid that came with my turkey frying pot. You'll also need a 25-inch-long piece of heavy-duty aluminum foil **H**, a handful of hardwood chips (apple might be nice), and the charcoal grate from the bottom of a standard Weber kettle grill. This wonderful 13½-inch-diameter multitasker is available at most hardware stores.

SMOKE THE APPLES

1. Fold the foil as seen in the sketches.

2. Deposit ½ cup hardwood chips to the center of the foil "smoke flower" and set this in the bottom of the wok.

3. Place the grill grate in the wok and load up the apple slices in a single layer.

4. Position the lid, set over a medium-high flame, and turn on your exhaust fan.

5. When you see a bit of smoke wisp out, drop the flame to medium and time for 30 minutes. Bingo, smoked apples.

PREPARE THE FONDUE

1. Combine the Cheddar and Velveeta in the bowl of a food processor. Process for 5 minutes, or until the cheese is smooth.*

2. Add the half-and-half, applejack and cayenne and again process until smooth.

3. Pulse in the smoked apple slices.

4. Serve immediately with the apple slices, celery, pretzels, cooked sausage, toasted pumpernickel or very small rocks. It can also be used as a sandwich spread or a "frosting" for corn bread. That's right, I said frosting.

Note: Due to the chemical composition of Velveeta, the dip will remain spreadable at room temperature for approximately 183 Earth days. If refrigerated, bring back to room temp prior to serving.

* This isn't so much about blending as it is using the heat from the motor to melt the cheese.

Chocolate Chess Pie

One 9-inch unbaked piecrust
   (I will allow store-bought)

16 ounces sugar

2 ounces unsweetened Dutch-process
   cocoa powder

2 teaspoons kosher salt

4 large eggs

1 5-ounce can evaporated milk

8 ounces (2 sticks) unsalted butter,
   melted

1 tablespoon vanilla extract

MERINGUE TOPPING
(OPTIONAL BUT STRONGLY URGED)

8 ounces sugar

2 ounces light corn syrup

4 ounces egg whites

1 teaspoon vanilla extract

1 cup finely chopped pecans, toasted

Etymological theories abound regarding this pie, with its sweet, eggy filling and little if any starch. One argument says "chess" is actually a lazy pronunciation of "chest" and refers to the "pie chests" where pies such as these were often housed. Skimpy, but I'll go with it. What I do know is that this is the best chocolate pie I've ever tasted, so I figure why not put a meringue on it? And as a nod to the most famous of all chess pies, pecan pie, why not put some pecans in the meringue?

1. Heat the oven to 375°F.

2. Line a 10-inch deep-dish (2 inches) tart pan with the piecrust. Be sure to press the dough into the sides and that there are no cracks or holes in the dough. Once assembled, chill the crust while you make the filling.

3. Combine the sugar, cocoa, salt, eggs, evaporated milk, butter and vanilla in your blender carafe and blend until smooth, about 1 minute. Pour the filling into the prepared piecrust.

4. Bake for 30 to 35 minutes, until the edges are set but the middle still has a bit of wobble to it. Cool for at least 1 hour before beginning the meringue.

5. To make the meringue, combine the sugar, corn syrup and 2 ounces water in a small saucepan. Cover and place over medium heat. Once boiling, uncover, clip on a candy thermometer **H** and bring the mixture to 240°F.

6. While the sugar syrup is cooking, whisk the egg whites and vanilla to medium peaks with a stand mixer fitted with the whisk attachment on high speed, 2 to 3 minutes.

7. With the mixer on low, pour the hot sugar syrup into the egg whites. Return the mixer to high speed after all of the sugar syrup has been added and whip to stiff peaks.

8. Fold the chopped pecans into the finished meringue. Dollop the finished meringue onto the cooled pie and use a blowtorch **H** to brown the meringue before serving.

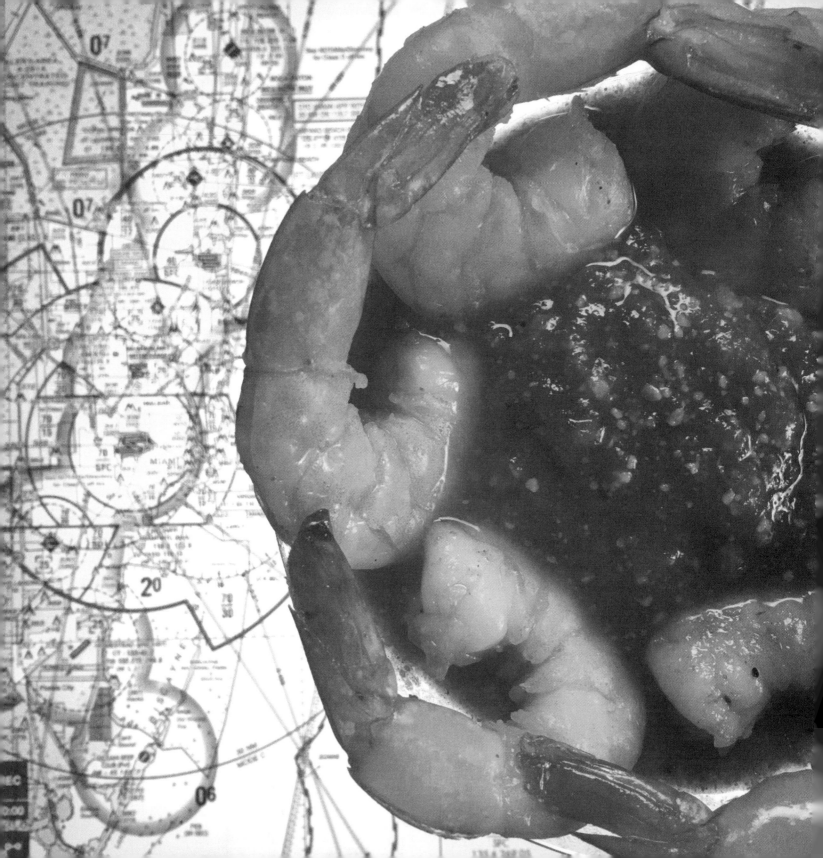

Cockpit Shrimp Cocktail

FEEDS 4 TO 6

I've spent a considerable amount of time in cramped cockpits wishing for a decent snack, especially something classy and flavorful like . . . shrimp cocktail. *Mmmmm.* The challenge is that up at altitude, even in a pressurized cabin, flavors get muddy and dull, which is why so much of what is served in airliners is so salty. So, I decided to come up with a shrimp cocktail that actually tastes like something at twenty-three thousand feet. And it tastes pretty good on the ground too.

There's a secret ingredient in the sauce: smoked almonds. Trust me.

SAUCE

¼ cup smoked almonds

1 28-ounce can whole tomatoes, drained

½ cup ketchup (I prefer Heinz, and no . . . they don't pay me to say that)

3 tablespoons sambal oelek chili paste

3 tablespoons prepared horseradish

1 tablespoon fresh lime juice

1 tablespoon Old Bay Seasoning

1 teaspoon dark brown sugar

2 tablespoons Worcestershire sauce

1 teaspoon kosher salt, optional

SHRIMP

2 ounces kosher salt

2 ounces granulated sugar

8 ounces ice cubes

1½ pounds (21/25 count) head-on, tail-on shrimp

1 tablespoon olive oil

1 teaspoon Old Bay Seasoning

1. To make the sauce, pulse the almonds in a food processor until the pieces resemble coarse meal. Then add the tomatoes, ketchup, sambal, horseradish, lime juice, Old Bay, brown sugar and Worcestershire sauce, and pulse to the desired consistency (I like mine a little on the chunky side).

2. Refrigerate for at least 3 hours, then taste and add the salt if desired.

3. To make the shrimp, combine 1 cup room-temperature water, the salt and granulated sugar in a large bowl and stir to dissolve. Add the ice and set aside. Use a pair of kitchen shears **H** to remove the veins from the shrimp without removing the head or the shell. Transfer the shrimp to the brine and refrigerate for 20 to 30 minutes.

4. Heat the broiler to its highest setting. Place a half sheet pan about 8 inches under the broiler for 5 minutes.

5. Drain the shrimp and rinse under cold water. Lay out on paper towels and pat dry. Toss with the olive oil and Old Bay. Arrange the shrimp in a single layer on the sizzling-hot sheet pan and slide it back under the broiler for 2 minutes. Meanwhile, clean out the bowl and stick it in the freezer. Flip the shrimp quickly with tongs **H** and return to the broiler for 1 more minute.

6. Transfer the shrimp to the chilled bowl and toss a few times to knock down the heat. Place in the freezer, tossing every few minutes for about 15 minutes, or until thoroughly chilled.

7. Peel the shrimp and serve with the cocktail sauce.

St. Louis Ribs

1½ teaspoons whole black peppercorns

1 teaspoon coriander seeds

1 teaspoon cumin seeds

2 teaspoons paprika

1 teaspoon onion powder

1 teaspoon garlic powder

¼ teaspoon freshly grated nutmeg **P**

¼ teaspoon cayenne pepper

3 slabs St. Louis–style pork ribs (2 to 3 pounds each)

¼ cup kosher salt

⅓ cup spicy brown mustard

SPECIAL EQUIPMENT

Smoker, 4 ounces hickory or oak wood chunks or chips

Spareribs that have had the skirt flap and tips removed. When smoking ribs, I always ask my butcher for St. Louis-style. She likes that about me.

Although I'll eat these ribs at any time of day, I'm especially drawn to them at the midnight hour. It's like they have a tiny voice, the siren song of which I can detect only when my apartment is quiet. And so I go to them, without even turning on a light. I like them hot on the outside but kinda cold on the inside, so sometimes when I'm working late or can't sleep, I unwrap them straight from the fridge and give them a quick hit with a blowtorch **H**. Romantic . . . no?

1. Heat a smoker to 225°F.

2. Combine the peppercorns, coriander seeds and cumin seeds in a blade-style spice/coffee grinder and buzz until coarse but even. Add the paprika, onion powder, garlic powder, nutmeg and cayenne. Buzz for 30 seconds, or until a fine powder is produced.

3. Pat the ribs dry and turn bone-side up. Remove the membrane on the underside of the ribs by inserting an upside-down spoon between the membrane and the meat at one end of the slab. Carefully work the spoon under the membrane to loosen but not tear. Once enough has been loosened, use a paper towel to grasp the membrane and slowly pull it down the slab to remove. If you skip this step, the connective tissue will shrink up during cooking and . . . well, you'll be sorry.

4. Season the ribs on both sides with the salt, brush both sides with the mustard, then sprinkle two thirds of the spice mixture on the meat side of the ribs and the remaining third on the bone side. Allow the ribs to sit at room temperature for about 30 minutes.

5. Once your smoker has reached 225°F, add the wood chips (or chunks, depending on model) and load in the ribs.

6. Cook the ribs for 4 to 5 hours, then test for doneness via these three criteria:

- The internal temperature of the meat should be 185° to 190°F.
- Pick up each slab from the center with tongs **H**. If done, said slab will droop into a U shape and crack slightly.
- The meat should not fall off the bone but should pull away with minimum pressure.

7. If the ribs pass the tests, remove them from the smoker, wrap in heavy-duty aluminum foil **H** and rest for at least 15 minutes. If not done, continue smoking for 30 minutes, then test again. Eventually, you'll get there.

Note: I always smoke extra slabs that I just leave wrapped in the foil to cool, then refrigerate so they're ready for late-night noshing. If you want them heated through, just move the pack onto a sheet pan (in case of leaks) and heat in a 300°F oven.

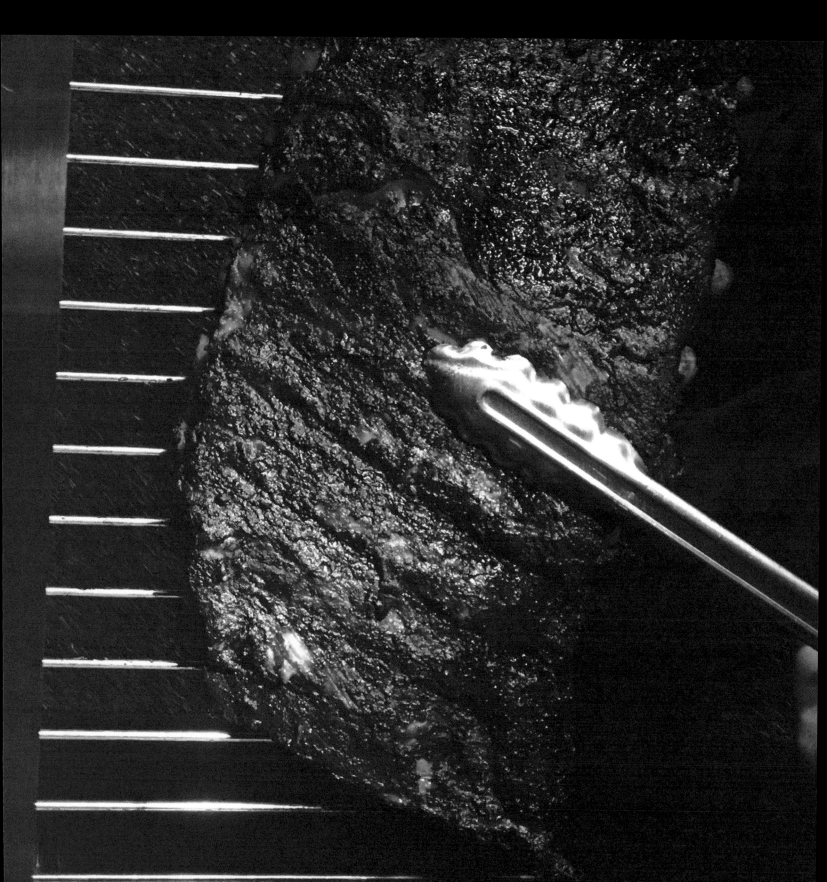

Fried Rice

FEEDS 4

4 ounces firm tofu

2 teaspoons sesame oil

1 pint cold cooked rice, preferably takeout

2 scallions, sliced

4 ounces shelled edamame, thawed if frozen

2 tablespoons soy sauce

2 tablespoons chili paste, such as sambal oelek chili paste

1 cup fresh basil leaves, shredded

SPECIAL EQUIPMENT

Steel wok **H** (available at just about any Asian market) and something really hot to put it on. This simply can't be done on an electric cooktop, and don't let anyone tell you otherwise. One of the flavors we're out for here is called *wok hei* and it's the charred flavor that comes from cooking in a rocket-hot wok. Although a strong gas burner is fine, what I like to do is load up a charcoal chimney starter **M** half full, light it, get it good and hot and park the wok right on top.

I wonder how many pint-size paper cartons of leftover Chinese restaurant take-out rice are thrown away a year. Doesn't matter. That's over now.

1. Cut the tofu into ½-inch slices and wrap in three layers of paper towels. Then, sandwich the bundle between two plates, set a 28-ounce can of tomatoes on top and leave at room temperature for 30 minutes. Unwrap and cube.

2. Heat the wok as hot as you can get it. If you turn off the lights, the bottom should glow . . . I'm not kidding.

3. When the wok is very hot, add the sesame oil (there will be smoke) and swirl to coat the pan. Immediately add the cold rice and fry, moving constantly, for 2 minutes, or until the rice is golden.

4. Add the tofu, scallions and edamame and fry for another 2 minutes, or until the scallions wilt.

5. Add the soy sauce, chili paste and basil and fry for 1 minute more. Serve immediately.

Midnight Mug Cake for 2

75 grams bittersweet chocolate, chopped

34 grams whole milk

⅛ teaspoon vanilla extract

Pinch of cayenne pepper

6 grams vegetable or canola oil (1 tablespoon)

36 grams sugar (4 tablespoons)

2 large eggs

29 grams all-purpose flour (3 tablespoons)

¼ teaspoon baking powder

Everything is mixed in the mug. I roll a very skinny whisk between my hands like a Boy Scout starting a fire; that way you get maximum mixing with minimum messing. You could get by with a fork, but it's going to take longer. Of course, if you have one of those little cappuccino frother wand things . . . we're done, personally.

1. Place the chocolate and milk in a 16-ounce mug and microwave on high for 45 seconds, then whisk until smooth. Add the vanilla, cayenne, vegetable oil and sugar and whisk smooth again.

2. Whisk in the eggs, then add the flour and baking powder and mix just until the batter comes together.

3. Place the mug on a paper plate  or towel (a little batter almost always spills over). Place in the center of the microwave and just let it sit for 3 minutes. (This will give the baking powder time to go to work.) Finally, microwave on high for 1:15. Be sure to watch as the batter sets and rises soufflélike right up and out of the mug like the mighty tower of chocolate goodness that it is.

4. When the microwave stops, the column will fall (that's okay, it happens to everybody). Turn out onto a plate or bowl and allow to cool briefly before splitting and filling with a scoop of vanilla ice cream.

Note: It's not pretty, but neither am I this time of night.

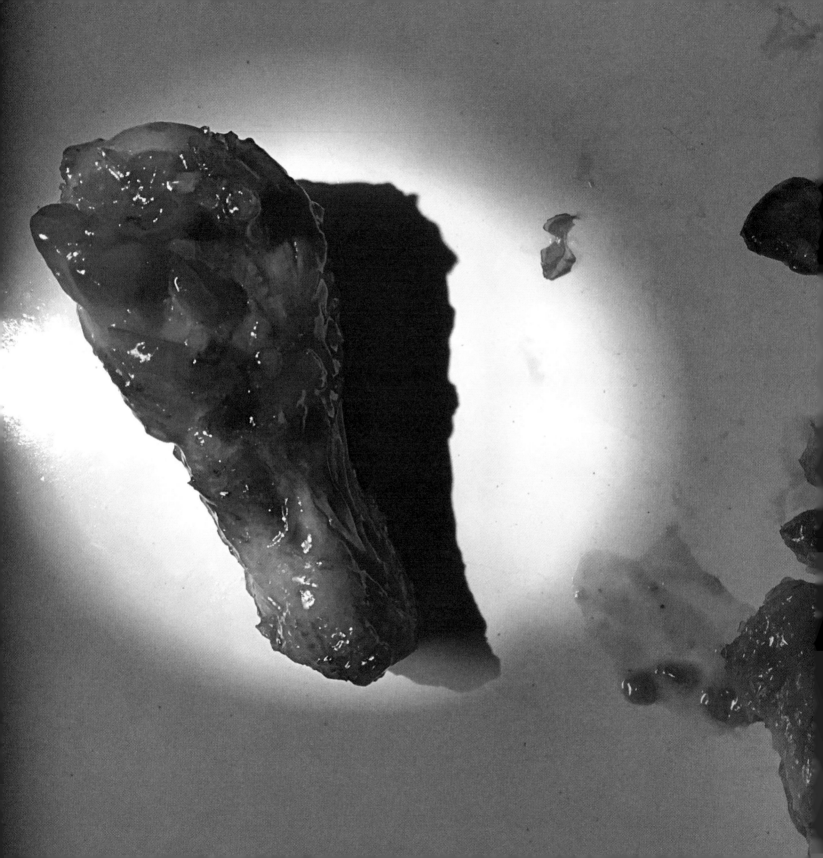

Chili-Glazed Wings

FEEDS 6

24 chicken wing drumettes

1 cup sweet Thai chili sauce, such as
    Mae Ploy

¼ cup rice wine or apple cider vinegar

⅓ cup Dr Pepper (trust me on this)

Kosher salt

Being bar food, most chicken wings are deep-fried, because deep-frying is fast and tasty, and most bars that serve food have commercial fryers. I would argue, however, that deep-frying is not the best way to cook chicken wings because they already contain enough fat to . . . wait for it . . . fry themselves!

But that in and of itself poses a problem, because if we roast the wings in the oven at a temperature sufficient to crisp the skin, we will produce a cloud of acrid, tear-inducing smoke that will stink up the house for days, not to mention summon anger in that round thing on the ceiling with the green eye and annoying chirp.

The answer: Steam them first. Sure, it's an extra step, but you'll be rewarded with crisp skin, perfectly done meat and a smoke-free kitchen.

Whenever I have to reduce a liquid by a specific fraction, as in this case, I stick a stainless steel ruler **H** right down the inside of the pot and measure the starting depth. That way, no matter the actual volume, I can get the percent of reduction right. Of course, working with a narrow vessel makes it a lot easier, but it also tends to slow down the reduction a bit.

1. Place a folding steamer basket **H** in the bottom of a stockpot and add enough water to come up not quite to the bottom of the steamer. Arrange the wings on the steamer like spokes on a wheel, with the large meaty ends pointing out and the bony narrow bits pointing in. If you're working with a standard steamer basket, you'll have to work in two batches. Cover the pot and bring to a boil over high heat. When steam comes out from under the lid, reduce the heat to medium and steam the wings for 10 minutes.

2. Remove the wings from the basket with your trusty tongs **H** and lay the wings out on a cooling rack set in a half sheet pan lined with paper towels. Refrigerate for 1 hour minimum. If working in batches, make sure chill time is 1 hour from the last batch.

3. Heat the oven to 425°F.

4. Bring the chili sauce, vinegar and Dr Pepper to a boil in a small saucepan over medium heat and reduce to a glaze consistency, about one third the original volume.

5. Remove the paper towels from the half sheet pan (leave the wings on the cooling rack and return the rack to the half sheet pan before baking) and bake the wings for 20 minutes. Transfer the wings to a large bowl and toss with the glaze. Return the wings to the pan and roast for another 10 minutes.

6. Arrange on a platter, sprinkle with salt to taste and serve with plenty of napkins.

From Page No. 64

MAKES 36 COOKIES

172 grams 54 percent bittersweet chocolate (6 ounces), coarsely chopped

56 grams unsweetened chocolate (2 ounces), coarsely chopped

52 grams all-purpose flour ($1^3/_4$ ounces)

$^1/_2$ teaspoon baking powder

$^1/_2$ teaspoon kosher salt

2 large eggs, at room temperature

1 teaspoon vanilla extract

56 grams unsalted butter (4 tablespoons/$^1/_2$ stick), at room temperature

172 grams light brown sugar (6 ounces)

86 grams 70 percent bittersweet chocolate (3 ounces), coarsely chopped

86 grams 40 percent milk chocolate (3 ounces), coarsely chopped

56 grams cocoa nibs (2 ounces)

The goal was simple: Pack more chocolate into a cookie than had ever been packed before. Each of these obsidian disks contains five forms of chocolate, which pretty much kicks the choco-crap out of any other cookie out there.

As always, where measuring matters most, I've gone to grams.

1. Place the 54 percent bittersweet chocolate and unsweetened chocolate in a heatproof bowl and microwave on high for two 30-second intervals, stirring after each interval. If it is still not smooth, heat for 10 additional seconds at a time and stir until it is. Set aside for about 15 minutes, until cooled to 90°F.

2. Whisk the flour, baking powder and salt together in a small bowl, then transfer to a paper plate . In the same bowl, whisk the eggs and vanilla together and set aside.

3. Mount the paddle attachment on a stand mixer and cream the butter and brown sugar on medium for about 2 minutes, until the mixture looks like wet sand.

4. Reduce the speed to low and slowly add the egg mixture until fully incorporated. Pour in the melted chocolate and mix to combine, stopping to scrape down the sides of the bowl as needed.

Then, with the mixer still on low, work in the flour mixture. When the batter seems homogenized, mix in the 70 percent bittersweet chocolate, milk chocolate and cocoa nibs.

5. Cover the bowl with plastic wrap and refrigerate for 45 minutes.

6. Heat the oven to 350°F. Line two half sheet pans with parchment paper.

7. Scoop the dough onto the prepared pans using a $1^1/_4$-inch-diameter disher or ice cream scoop, placing the mounds 2 inches apart for 12 cookies per pan. Bake for 8 to 9 minutes, rotating the pans after 5 minutes. The cookies may still look a bit wet when they come out, but that's okay.

8. Cool the cookies on the pan for 2 minutes, then slide the parchment paper to a rack to let the cookies cool completely. Repeat steps 7 and 8 with remaining dough.

To Page No. 173

Witnessed / Reviewed & Understood by me,   Date   Entered by: Date
        12/14/15

MOTOR.

ONLY ONE PAIR OF THESE SHOES
EVER MADE.

nning a sewing
. The motor is
a starting rod
lowing the ma-
the feet of the
are secured ac-

A style of foot gear, unlike anything
ever worn before in the history of the
world, has just appeared in the shape of
what is called "twenty-strap sandals," a
pair of which were made especially for
Anne Held. They cost

The electric sewing
machine is an interesting
example of "production

this . . .
for her
. . . a
Florenz
all these
make
a darling of
was born in
e to the
es in 1896
in plays like
n Model,
and A Parlor
orced from
1915, she
Paris, where
1918

City inventor
inciple

Open Sesame Noodles

1 cup rice wine vinegar

½ cup sugar

1 teaspoon kosher salt

½ teaspoon red pepper flakes **P**

1 hothouse English cucumber

284 grams smooth peanut butter

40 grams soy sauce

15 grams plus 2 tablespoons toasted
    sesame oil

25 grams sambal chili paste (sambal
    oelek is what I keep on hand)

20 grams freshly grated ginger (about
    a finger's worth)

30 grams rice wine vinegar*

20 grams sugar (about 1 tablespoon)

10 ounces dry pasta, cooked al dente
    (see Cold Water Pasta Method **M**) or
    1 pound fresh Chinese egg noodles,
    cooked according to package
    directions**

(As in open the refrigerator door in the middle of the night and eat them right out of the container, standing there pretty much naked.)

Note: Although this recipe makes plenty of sauce for two, you may want to go as much as triple here so that you can keep some refrigerated in a jar for next time.

1. Combine the rice wine vinegar, sugar, salt and red pepper flakes in a mixing bowl. Mix well then add the sliced cucumber. Cover with plastic wrap and set aside in the fridge while you prepare the sauce.

2. Install the standard blade in the work bowl of your food processor, then put the work bowl on your scale **H**. Weigh in the peanut butter, soy sauce, 15 grams toasted sesame oil, chili paste, ginger, rice wine vinegar and sugar. Remember to zero out the weight of each ingredient as you go. This is one of those cases where the scaling is more about convenience than precision, so if you are a gram or two on either side of target, it's okay. The sauce won't explode or anything.

3. Run the food processor steady for about 2 minutes. Scrape down the sides, if needed, and go for another minute, or until the sauce is smooth.

4. Toss the cooked noodles with the remaining 2 tablespoons of sesame oil in a large bowl. Add ¾ of the peanut sauce and toss in the noodles until thoroughly coated (you can add more sauce as desired or save the rest for another day). This is a lot easier if the sauce is warm, so if you're getting it out of the fridge, you may want to nuke it briefly.

5. Garnish with the pickled cucumber and devour.

6. Wash your face, you disgusting animal!

* Rice vinegar and rice wine vinegar are the same thing. The real differences come when color is involved. Although Japanese styles are generally white, Chinese styles include white, black and red, depending on the color of the rice from which they're made. I typically use red for this dish, but if all you have is a light Japanese version, use that. But do not use a "seasoned" vinegar made for sushi; it's got a lot of salt and sugar added to it.

** Classically, this dish is made with fresh or even frozen Chinese egg noodles, which are pretty easy to find in Chinese markets. But, for me at least, this is an impulse dish. I keep the sauce in a jar in the fridge so that I can throw this together with any kind of noodles from spaghetti to instant ramen. Last time I made it I used number 15 perciatelli. The key is to cook the noodle al dente, then immediately rinse with cold water, drain, then lube with toasted sesame oil. Skip that and the noodles will be gummy no matter what.

Jungle Bird

1 cup ice cubes

1½ ounces rum **B**

1½ ounces pineapple juice

¾ ounce Cocchi Rosa Americano **B**

½ ounce fresh lime juice

½ ounce simple syrup

2-inch cube of ice

Pineapple wedge or skewer

Freshly grated nutmeg **P**

Pinch of kosher salt

Although its inventor, who was working in a bar in Kuala Lumpur in the early seventies, chose to create this tiki classic with Campari **B**, I prefer Cocchi* Rosa Americano, an apéritif composed of a blend of wines punched up with various fruits, herbs and spices, including cinchona bark, whose quinine provides Cocchi's bark, so to speak. The nutmeg and a pinch of salt round out the flavors and keep the bitter and sweet from killing each other.

1. Combine the ice cubes, rum, pineapple juice, Cocchi, lime juice and simple syrup in the bottom of a Boston-style shaker. Cover and shake for 15 to 30 seconds, until chilled and frothy.

2. Strain the rum mixture into an old-fashioned glass over the 2-inch cube of ice. Garnish with pineapple, nutmeg and salt. Serve immediately.

* Pronounced "cokey."

Tomorrow, French Fries

FEEDS 4

These are not baked french fries but rather baked potatoes turned into french fries. The miracle here (if I may call it that) is that this process allows you to skip the double frying called for by most french fry recipes. And, since the spuds are already cooked when they go into the oil, there's very little of the foaming and boiling over that can be experienced with raw potatoes. The only downside is you have to bake the potatoes today for frying tomorrow, hence the name.

4 russet potatoes (about 8 ounces each),
    scrubbed and rinsed
2 teaspoons plus 2 quarts peanut oil
Kosher salt

1. Bake the potatoes at least 12 hours in advance: Position a rack in the top half of the oven with a half sheet pan on the rack below. Heat the oven to 350°F.

2. Poke a few deep holes in the potatoes with a fork or paring knife. Coat each potato lightly with the 2 teaspoons of the peanut oil and sprinkle generously with salt.

3. Bake directly on the oven rack for 45 minutes to 1 hour, until tender.

4. Cool to room temperature and then refrigerate overnight.

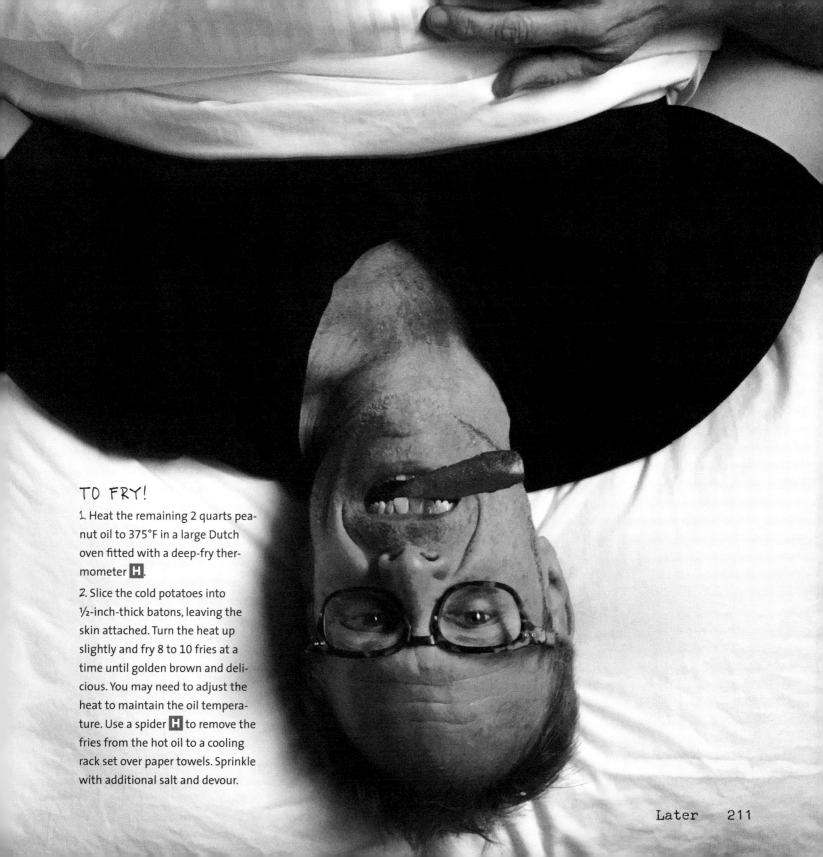

TO FRY!

1. Heat the remaining 2 quarts peanut oil to 375°F in a large Dutch oven fitted with a deep-fry thermometer **H**.

2. Slice the cold potatoes into ½-inch-thick batons, leaving the skin attached. Turn the heat up slightly and fry 8 to 10 fries at a time until golden brown and delicious. You may need to adjust the heat to maintain the oil temperature. Use a spider **H** to remove the fries from the hot oil to a cooling rack set over paper towels. Sprinkle with additional salt and devour.

RECIPES BY CATEGORY

RECITES BY METHOD

BAKE
Amaranth Wafers 42
Apple Spice Bundt Cake with Rum
  Glaze 46
Blueberry Pound Cake 8
Bourbon Bread Pudding 128
Brown on Blonde 93
Chewy Peanut Butter Cookie 97
Chocapocalypse Cookie 204
Chocolate Chess Pie 193
Corn Bread 32
"EnchiLasagna" or "Lasagnalada" 78
Hot Saltine Hack 170
Little Brown Biscuits 17
Oatmeal Banana Bread 12
Peach "Cobbles" 40

BLACKEN
BCLT Tacos (Blackened Catfish Lettuce
  Tomato) 15

BOIL
Always Perfect Oatmeal 4
Barley Water 183
Black-Eyed Peas 32
Breakfast Carbonara 2
Butterscotch Puddin' 90
Fiery Ginger Ale Concentrate 110
Grits with Shrimp 18
Open Sesame Noodles 206
Pho Bo (Beef Pho) 11
Preserved Lemons–ade 167
Pumpkin Cheesecake 145
Salty Chocolaty Peanut Buttery
  Crunchy Bars 172
Thai Iced Tea 98

Weeknight Spaghetti 139
Zissou's Buffet of Underwater
  Delights 107

BLEND
Buttermilk Lassi 7
Cider House Fondue 191
Kick-in-the-Pants Smoothie 94
Pâté de Sardine 168
Seedy Date Bars 36

BRAISE
Onion Oxtail Soup 114

BROIL
Chilaquiles! 21
Mr. Crunchy 27

CREAM WHIPPER
Cream Whipper Chocolate Mousse
  141
Nitrous Pancakes 25

EMULSIFY
Scrambled Eggs V3.0 28

DEEP-FRY
BBQ Potato Chips 54
Beale Street Cheeseburger 64
Oyster Po'boy 81
The General's Fried Chicken 164
Tomorrow, French Fries 210

FREEZE
Cucumber Lime Yogurt Pops 108
Peach Punch Pops 162
Watermelon Campari Sorbet 188

GRILL
Chuan'r 187
Garam Masalmon Steaks 142
Grilled Cheese Grilled Sandwich 53
Grilled Shishitos 175
Grilled Squid Salad 158
Turkey Tikka Masala 155

MICROWAVE
Midnight Mug Cake for 2 200

NO-COOK
Bad Day Bitter Martini 130
Cocoa Nib Vinaigrette 118
Cold Brew Coffee 39
Green Grape Cobbler 88
Iceberg Slaw 81
Jungle Bird 209
My Big Fat Greek Chicken Salad 56
Not Just Another Kale Salad 84
Overnight Coconut Oats 22
Quick Preserved Lemons 167
Red, Red Wine (Sangria) 105
Savory Greek Yogurt Dip 100
Smoky Tequila Sour 150
Tossed Beet Salad 60

PANFRY
Black Beans/Brown Rice 75
Char-Burgers 133
Chicken Parmesan Balls 76
Chicken Piccata 117
Fish Sticks and Custard 73
Kimchi Crab Cakes 121
Mushroom Stroganoff 153
Salisbury Steak 147

Turkey Sliders 63

PANINI
Totally Panini-Pressed Dinner 156

PRESSURE
Mushroom Wheat Berry Pilaf 61
No-Can Tomato Soup 52
The Greens 30

ROAST
Cockpit Shrimp Cocktail 195
Crispy Chickpeas 102
Heavenly Orbs of Belgian Goodness
  137
Lacquered Bacon 45
One Pot Chicken 134
Roast Broccoli Hero 68
Roasted Chile Salsa 176
Roasted Thanksgiving Salad 71
Snapper-Dome 149
The Final Turkey 82
The Last Pizza Dough I'll Ever Need
  180

SMOKE
Barbecue Pork Butt 124
Smoky the Meat Loaf 67
St. Louis Ribs 196

STEAM
Chili-Glazed Wings 203
Mussels-O-Miso 126

WOK
Fried Rice 199

INDEX

Page numbers of photographs appear in italics.

BY ALTON BROWN